C000232370

# THE PIERROTS OF THE YORKSHIRE COAST

by

## Mave and Ben Chapman

HUTTON PRESS

1988

Published by the Hutton Press Ltd.
130 Canada Drive, Cherry Burton, Beverley
East Yorkshire HU17 7SB

Copyright © 1988

No part of this book may be reproduced, stored in a retrieval system
or transmitted in any form, or by any means electronic, mechanical,
photocopying, recording or otherwise without the prior permission
of the Publisher and the Copyright holders.

*Printed and Bound by*

*Clifford Ward & Co. (Bridlington) Ltd.*
*55 West Street, Bridlington, East Yorkshire*
*YO15 3DZ*

ISBN 0 907033 70 9

*For*
*Chas and Tommy*
*- A hard act to follow -*

# CONTENTS

# FOREWORD
(by the Northern theatrical historian, Geoff J. Mellor)


Around 25 years ago the late Harry J. Scott - then Editor of the Dalesman Magazine - asked me to write about "the Pierrots".

It transpired the magazine had received a number of readers' letters on the subject, mostly the nostalgic memories of elderly people, lamenting the changes at the seaside resorts and especially the passing of "the Pierrots".

With my rather specialised knowledge of the Northern entertainment scene, Mr. Scott thought that I was "just the person to do some research on the subject and put the Pierrot letters into book form".

Apparently no one had written seriously about "the Pierrots" before and the idea appealed to him. It also appealed to me, as a challenge.

Also, I was very friendly with Alan Gale (now sadly no longer with us) who claimed to be the last man to promote and run an open-air Pierrot show at the seaside. This was at Redcar in 1950, after which Mr. Gale left to organise entertainments in connection with the Festival of Britain, held in London during 1951.

And so, after consultation with Alan Gale and other ex-Pierrots around in the Sixties - together with much patient research - the little book *Pom-Poms and Ruffles* was eventually written. This was published in 1966 as a glossy paperback, with illustrations, at the incredible price of six shillings (30p.), and is now a collector's item.

I know Mave and Ben Chapman are keen collectors of Pierrot postcards and photographs, and it was with pleasure that I learned my *Pom-Poms and Ruffles* had inspired them to delve deeply and write about the Pierrots of the Yorkshire Coast in depth.

In other words, to continue the good work, and stimulate interest in an old-fashioned but much loved form of entertainment, now gone forever.

It is right that those unsung heroes of alfresco seaside shows should be remembered. I wish the new book every success.

GEOFF J. MELLOR

7

# ACKNOWLEDGEMENTS

We wish to acknowledge the generous help afforded to us by the following:-

Geoff Mellor, who has written our Foreword. It was his book *Pom Poms and Ruffles* which inspired us to embark upon our own research and produce a detailed study of the pierrots in our particular area. We would also like to thank him for his encouragement and generous help with information.

Mary Williams of Redcar. Without her wide-ranging assistance we would not have been able to produce such a comprehensive account of the entertainment scene in the Cleveland area.

Doris Beanland of Canada, who provided family background material, anecdotes and press cuttings about her husband's family, the Beanlands, well known for their shows in Bridlington.

Allan Russell who shared with us memories of his father and mother and thereby helped us to produce our account of the Hornsea troupe.

Veronica Twidle of Redcar for helpful suggestions and invaluable addresses for furthering our research.

Jenny Church of Hull, for memories of her father Charles Milner during his successful years at Withernsea.

Jean Atkinson for her memories of the Jovial Jollies.

Mrs V. Alexander and Mr Dennis Wright of Redcar, both of whom took time and trouble to give us very full accounts of entertainments in their area.

We would also like to thank the following people for their efforts on our behalf. Irene Lawson and Molly Lawton of Withernsea; Ken Marshall of Cleveland; Leslie Frost of Sheffield; Muriel Kirk of the Holderness Gazette for help with research and loan of material; Mavis Barrick of Withernsea Library; Anne Willey and Jill Crowther of Hull Reference and Local Studies Libraries for assistance with research. Pauline, Iris and Jean of Bridlington, the Bed and Breakfast Belles who were extremely helpful; Mary Carmichael of Hollym; Valerie Harrison of Hull; Nancy Goldthorpe of Wakefield; Brian Boyce and Jean May, postcard dealers of Hull who diligently searched for some of the rarer photographs in our archives.

We also acknowledge valuable help from the following newspapers and institutions: Yorkshire Post, Scarborough Mercury, Cleveland Clarion, Bridlington Free Press, Holderness Gazette, Whitby Gazette, Hull Star.

Scarborough Library, Redcar Library, Withernsea Library, Hornsea Museum Whitby Literary and Philosophical Society.

Our thanks also to all the many people who have written to us with information in response to our appeals over the last five years.

A special thanks to our niece Jane Conroy, our ever willing chauffeur who conveyed us around in our efforts to track down elusive material.

The illustrations are from the extensive collection of alfresco entertainment photographs which form part of the Chapman Social History Archive.

Mave and Ben Chapman
Withernsea
May 1988

# INTRODUCTION

In the mid nineteenth century when Queen Victoria ascended the throne, seaside holidays were a pleasure and a luxury confined to the rich and fashionable.

Britain was then enjoying a period of industrial expansion, and the middle classes were beginning to take a share in the nation's prosperity. This combined with the development of a wider railway system opened up the facility of travel to include the coastal resorts; consequently seaside holidays became a regular feature in the lives of middle class families and their households.

Housemaids, nannies and kitchen staff all accompanied the family to the seaside. The popular practice at this time was to rent a large house for a period of four or five months during the summer season, at a resort not too far removed from one's permanent home. The house selected was usually taken year after year by the same family. Mother and any small children would spend the whole season there, ably supported by nannie and other servants. Sometimes she enjoyed the company of aunts, cousins or other female relatives. Older children arrived when the boarding schools closed for the summer. Fathers, uncles and the male cousins spent their weekends at the coast with the family, returning to their business on Mondays. They usually managed a full week or two during the season away from their labours.

The servants, in view of this arrangement, found themselves with more free time during the week than they would normally expect back at the town residence, although the weekends were often quite hectic with the whole family in residence. This meant that with the extra amount of leisure time available to them, they too could enjoy the diverse entertainments available to holiday-makers.

The enterprising railway companies introduced moderately priced day excursions to the resorts, which were extremely popular with the workers in the towns and industrial cities, especially in the north of England. The organisers of Sunday School outings and the like also took advantage of these generous terms.

Visitors to the resorts of all classes, whether their stay be of long or short duration, were eager for entertainment to enhance their enjoyment of the visit.

Originally there was an array of street performers including jugglers, street musicians with barrel organs and fiddlers, tumblers and singers. There was of course the ubiquitous Punch and Judy show.

With this period of prosperity came the establishment of the first resident seaside entertainers. The concert party tradition began with the popular "Nigger Minstrels", whose fast talking and naive form of entertainment had recently been introduced from America. By the 1860's most resorts had a Minstrel Show. They were all male shows, usually of a very high standard and appealed

9

*Victorian street entertainment.*

to young and old, rich or poor alike, extremely acccomplished instrumentalists and singers, whose faces were blackened with the aid of burnt cork. An integral member of each troupe was the "Uncle", who organised competitions for the children and other delights; consequently he became the idol of the resort for the season.

For almost three decades the minstrels dominated the beaches of the popular resorts, until in the 1890's a challenge came in the form of the pierrots. They were the antithesis of the minstrels, faces whitened with zinc oxide, attired in immaculate ruffled white suits with black pom poms, and about them an air of romance. For the following fifty years they formed the basis of seaside entertainment.

The pierrots were first introduced to England in 1891 by Clifford Essex. They possessed a certain refinement, lacking in their brash minstrel counterparts, which appealed particularly to the fairer sex. They became an immediate success, and within a short space of time, every seaside resort boasted at least one troupe. Often there was a choice, this rivalry enhancing the performances, and producing some very fine artists.

Originally the Pierrots gave their "shows" on what was termed their "pitch", an area on the beach. Some troupes laid down boards, others performed directly on the sand itself. In later years, as they became increasingly popular, they built open air stages or "alfrescos". The people would congregate round these stages, which were strategically placed to accommodate as many as possible. Some paid a nominal fee to sit in deck chairs and there were on occasions mats or forms at the front for children. A box would be passed round after the performance for any contributions, as a fee was usually levied by the local council for permission to use the beach.

The troupes supported themselves financially by an extremely skilful technique known as "bottling". A good "bottler" was a real asset to a troupe. He usually possessed great charm and charisma, which used to its full effect could extract that extra coin from a young lady's purse, as he passed with his box, or velvet bag on the end of a stick amongst the crowds around the stage and to those above on the pier or esplanade. The name "bottling" is belived to derive from the fact that the proceeds of the collections were placed in a bottle so that they were not easily removable. At the end of the week, the bottle was broken and the money shared out fairly among the members of the company.

It is with these hard working, dedicated troupes that this book is primarily concerned. They regularly gave four shows a day (on Bank Holidays five) in the most adverse of conditions. Not for them the comforts of the theatre dressing room; they faced the elements, be it blazing sunshine or pouring rain with stoic good humour and fortitude; the latter being responsible for the sad little notices, "If wet under the pier"!

These performers gave their best, and often for meagre financial return. It is a sad reflection on our times that they have now almost been forgotten. They gave to people of all ages and classes a kind of enjoyment rarely experienced today.

Inevitably, a more sophisticated approach became necessary, and the concert parties began to perform in the pier theatres and Floral Halls. These shows were often quite lavishly presented and were the forerunners of today's spectacular summer shows.

The artists who comprised the pierrot shows were an extremely versatile set, often capable of performing more than one type of act. Many of them eventually became household names, such as Arthur Askey, Wee Georgie Wood, Harry Korris, Max Miller, Jack Hylton, and Elsie and Doris Waters, to name but a few. Classic examples from our own region were Dickie Henderson senior and Bunny Doyle, nationally acclaimed Yorkshire comedians of the past.

Some of the more enterprising performers would inevitably break away from the confines of their troupe, and form new troupes of their own, using their experiences to the full; many proved to be very good managers.

During the First World War some performers sadly gave their lives for their country, others organised shows based on their peace time seaside experience, often substituting light hearted material with sardonic trench humour. Members of these troupes were often drawn from the ranks or on occasion were amateur performers who were recuperating from minor injuries.

We have been very fortunate and privileged to meet and talk to people who had relatives, or were themselves concerned with pierrot troupes in our region. Anecdotes told to us, and memories related of enjoyable pierrot performances are included in the text under the appropriate headings.

We feel honoured that many kind people have been willing to share their pleasant memories, and on occasion, family history with us. We have compiled this book specifically because we feel that these sterling performers have been sadly neglected, although much has been written and compiled *ad nauseam* on music hall performers of the same period.

The pierrot troupes were, of course, a national institution, but we have deliberately chosen to present to you the performers who appeared at our Yorkshire coast resorts from Redcar in the North down to Withernsea at the mouth of the Humber.

Mave and Ben Chapman

## AUTHORS' NOTE.

We have made no attempt to include every concert party that may have appeared on the Yorkshire coast during the first half of this century. Our aim has been to tell the story of the men who worked hard season after season to bring joy to the public. These men, and later women, were prepared to give of their best for very little reward, under less than ideal conditions. No doubt some of our readers will feel that there are omissions which were worthy of inclusion; to them we apologise, but this is our personal choice. Reasonable attempts have been made to trace all owners of copyright where applicable.

The authors would be pleased to hear from anyone on the subject of pierrots and concert parties from anywhere in Britain. We wish to maintain and expand our archives on this subject for posterity.

# REDCAR

Redcar, and Coatham, with which it is now joined, were old fishing villages. Like most of the resorts on the Yorkshire coast they rapidly developed into holiday towns primarily for the workers of the grimy industrial Teeside area. Until 1900 Redcar and Coatham were separate towns although only a few yards of land divided them, and were originally administered by different authorities. Today very few people are able to define the position of the original boundaries. Our Victorian ancestors being adept at producing structures of immense complexity seem to have developed a predilection for the construction of piers at seaside resorts. Both Redcar and Coatham decided that the building of a pier would enhance the attractions of their respective towns, Redcar two years before Coatham. Building of the pier at Redcar began in 1871 and the Grand Opening, a very festive occasion, took place at the Whitsuntide of 1873. Tragedy struck in 1880 when the pier was reduced in length due to the brig *Luna* colliding with it during a storm. It was again severely damaged by a storm in 1897 but the final ignominy was the fire which ravaged the remaining structure in 1898, completely burning it down. In 1909, a pavilion was erected at the shore end of the now ruined pier. This provided a venue for seaside shows for many years.

Coatham pier was begun in 1873 but appears to have been ill fated from the start. It too had the misfortune to be breached by a ship, whilst still under construction in December of 1874 during one of the worst storms the east coast has ever suffered. Dogged by adversity, its fate was sealed in 1898 when it again suffered a collision, was allowed to fall into disrepair, and was finally demolished in 1899. The shore end was used for many years as a pierrot pitch.

A magnificent beach sweeps from the mouth of the Tees towards Marske and Saltburn, and in its time has been the home of many forms of entertainment. There were swings and roundabouts for the children and over countless years the Sandcastle Competitions were a high spot of the season. These appear to have delighted the adults as much as the children. Ingenious structures were built as close to the promenade as possible to protect them from the tide. There were many towered castles with flags and soldiers on the battlements, churches with weddings of tiny dolls. One year a particularly enterprising local lad modelled a crocodile and covered it with mussel shells; it had a winking eye in the form of a small bulb operated by a torch battery. Cardboard box lids were often put out into which people threw pennies for the modellers. Some illuminated their efforts with candles in jam jars as the evenings grew dark. Then came the suspense of wondering if one had been lucky enough to win a prize.

Professor Will Fleet, the Punch and Judy man and Professor Foster, a ventriloquist, timed their shows so that the children could run from one to the other without missing a trick. There was also that great seaside institution, the patient donkeys.

The pierrots were a major source of enjoyment for both child and adult. There were troupes on the beach at Redcar from the 1880's through several decades until 1950.

The first pierrots to perform at Redcar were Johnny (Smiler) Grove's Troupe. Johnny was a Scarborough man who began his career as a seaside entertainer. He originally ran a black face minstrel show on Scarborough sands in the early 1890's when he was about twenty years of age. After a few seasons he left the beach and went on the Halls being particularly successful as a pantomime dame. Around the turn of the century he came to Redcar with a troupe of pierrots who performed on the site of the old bandstand. There were six members of this all male troupe, with the traditional suits, ruffles and pom poms. The star turn was a lanky comedian called "Weary Willie". In 1899 Marie Lloyd and Florrie Fords appeared on the beach at Redcar with "Smiler's" men. A damaged and somewhat faded photograph shows Marie and Florrie wearing dresses with ruffles and pom poms with a line up of the boys. It is not clear whether the ladies appeared on a single occasion (possibly a Gala night) or if they gave regular performances.

It was originally intended that Johnny Grove's Pierrots should entertain the old people of the town at a dinner in the Central Hall. The dinner was scheduled for June in honour of The Coronation of Edward VII. The Coronation, however, was postponed due to the indisposition of the King who had appendicitis and was unfit to attend the ceremony. By this time plans were so far advanced for the dinner that it was decided it should be held as arranged. Johnny and his troupe gave an enjoyable show long remembered by those present.

They stayed at Redcar for several seasons, and by 1907 had become Johnny Grove's Royal Entertainers, having performed for Royalty on one occasion. They now sported cropped, waist length jackets and white trousers with cummerbunds, topped with the popular straw boaters of the period. They retained their popularity despite the fact that other troupes were now appearing at Redcar to entertain the visitors.

Sam Paul and his Cleveland Cadets were popular with the Redcar audiences in the early years of the reign of George V, leading up to the First World War. They had their first show in the summer of 1910, and successive years until 1914.

Sam Paul was in fact Robert Nesbitt Sample. In the 1910 season he and his wife Florence were living at number 42 Alfred Street in Redcar. During this time, on the 2nd of June 1910 his daughter, christened Florence after her mother, was born.

They performed all the popular songs of the day in an alfresco which was set up on the beach. Sam was born in 1833 and like many other performers of the east coast began his career as a pierrot with Will Catlin's troupe at Scarborough. There were eight Cadets who wore the now popular double-breasted blazers, white trousers and yachting caps. The climax of the show was a sketch which was always performed as a grand finale and so contrived as to include all the members of the troupe.

*Johnnie Groves's Royal Redcar Pierrots, 1904.*

*Sam Paul's Cleveland Cadets, 1911 (Sam is in the centre reading the newspaper).*

15

Sam and his men always gave a very late show on Friday evenings, which was intended for the local people after the trippers, wearied with the excitement of the day, had returned to the station and the homeward bound excursion trains.

This show was much appreciated by the landladies of the boarding houses, whose guests kept them busy through the week. On Friday nights they managed an hour or two of leisure as one lot of guests prepared for the journey home in the morning, and the new visitors were not expected to arrive until late afternoon.

During the 1913 season which was apparently memorable for the exceptionally hot weather, Sam's second daughter Margaret was born. He and Florence had by then moved to 3 Henry Street, Coatham.

Sam decided to venture into the realms of cinema and hired the Central Hall, which was built on the site of Redcar's first railway station. It was here that he opened his Picture Palace. He is said to have taught young George Formby to play the ukelele in the early 1920's. George originally appeared on the stage as George Hoy, using his mother's maiden name, but after the death of his father in 1921 he was eventually persuaded to use the name Formby. George's solo act in the Halls was not going at all well, so Sam Paul who was an expert on both banjo and ukelele, took him in hand. As a true friend he helped him with his gags and taught him to play the instrument. This set the pattern for George's very successful career.

By the summer of 1912 Bert Leighton and his Redcar Follies pierrot troupe were appearing on the beach. On Wednesday the 14th of August of that year, a most unseasonable storm occurred along the Cleveland coast. A heavy swell on the sea meant that the tide was exceptionally high for the time of year. Huge waves lashed the coast and a considerable amount of damage was done at Redcar. The men who operated the pleasure boats managed to secure their craft, but Bert Leighton and his troupe were not so fortunate. The afternoon performance was cut short when the incoming tide, which progressed with frightening rapidity, produced waves of astonishing height, crashing down onto the alfresco and wrecking it. Performers and audience scattered in all directions, the less able being drenched to the skin.

Sympathy for the pierrots was soon practically expressed. One or two well wishers went round with their hats asking "Who will help Mr. Leighton?"; the crowd gave generously.

It was impossible for the evening performance to be held on the beach, but the crowds followed the pierrots to Redcar Lane Gardens, where they played to a large audience who, no doubt gave very generously in appreciation of these brave fellows who put their hearts into a performance after such a shocking experience.

During the same season the audiences at the Pier Pavilion were being entertained by Mr. Frederick Lane's Kimonos Concert Party. Not only were they patronised by the visitors but were well supported by the residents of Redcar, having appeared on numerous occasions in previous seasons. They had established an excellent reputation for giving a top class performance. Obviously having the advantage of the Pavilion they fared somewhat better than poor Bert Leighton during the storm.

16

There were also the Scarleteers who were billed as Mr. C. Hinchcliffe's Vaudeville Company. They included Miss Jessie Ewart, Miss Lilian Voisey, Miss Mary Hope, Mr. Harry Turner, Mr. Sydney Lean and Harry S. Clarke, who also directed the show.

In 1913 the Waddlers were performing on the beach along with numerous other troupes. There was now quite a choice of entertainment on offer and competition for the favours of the audiences was keen.

This produced an extremely high standard of entertainment. It is difficult to assess without first-hand experience of the situation, but it has been suggested that the period directly preceding the First World War probably saw a standard of entertainment on the beaches of coastal resorts round the country which has never been equalled.

Jimmy Lynton was born on the 17th July 1887. In 1892, he made his first appearance as a child entertainer in pom poms and ruffles with Professor O'Dells's Royal Juvenile Pierrots. In his early days, Jimmy was a rover. He worked summer seasons in many parts of the country sometimes with his own troupe, and sometimes as a member of another troupe. It was whilst appearing at Filey with Andie Caine that Jimmy's son was born. Sadly he was reported missing, presumed dead, whilst serving with the R.A.F. during the Second World War. Jimmy was a comedian and character man and in the season of 1920 he appeared in Redcar with his own troupe, the Cosy Corner Pierrots. Towards the end of the decade, along with his wife Celia Ridgeway who was a soubrette, he joined Billy Scarrow, thus prolonging his association with Redcar. In his retirement he became a columnist for the trade newspaper, *The World's Fair*, the much loved organ of show people.

No account of beach entertainment at Redcar would be complete without a

*Billy Scarrow's Pierrots, 1927. From left: Jimmy Lynton,*
*Celia Ridgeway (Mrs Lynton), Billy Scarrow.*

mention of Sunshine Corner. This was situated at the end of the promenade not far from Billy Scarrow's pitch. A large slipway to the beach provided a convenient place for the audience. The show was run by Uncle Tom (no one seems to have known him by any other name) and his band of helpers. They sang songs which were presumably composed by Uncle Tom himself. There was a portable organ to provide accompaniment and the audience participated in a sing-along, complete with hand movements to illustrate the words. All the songs had a religious theme, and children were encouraged to go on to the stage and sing either a chorus or solo, for which they were rewarded with a stick of rock. This little group had a faithful following amongst the residents of Redcar, and often when pensioners get together for a social evening in the town today someone will start singing a chorus from the Sunshine Corner days. Soon everyone joins in complete with hand movements. A typical chorus to start the singing on the beach went thus:

> *Sunshine Corner, oh it's jolly fine,*
> *It's for children, under ninety nine.*
> *All are welcome, seats are given free*
> *Redcar Sunshine Corner is the place for me!*

A cheerful sentiment if not strictly true. Standing room was certainly free, but a seat had to be paid for. The entertainers, like their "bottling" brothers the pierrots, came round with a collecting box.

Perhaps the troupe which is best remembered today above all others in Redcar is Billy Scarrow's Optimists. Billy came to Redcar after the Armistice in 1918 and performed every season until the outbreak of war in 1939. Information concerning Billy Scarrow's background is sparse. We have been informed by a gentleman who met him that his father ran a fairground in Wales, and that Billy was a friend of the phenomenal young boxer Jimmy Wilde. We can find no record of stage appearances or performances with other pierrot troupes, but we find it difficult to believe that Billy, who had a first rate tenor voice, came to Redcar and formed the Optimists with no previous experience as an entertainer.

The Optimists were immensely popular; obviously over the years the troupe did have changes, but many of the artistes came back season after season and made firm friendships with the local people, often being invited into their homes. Like other troupes of the day they worked extremely hard, giving the usual three shows a day, weather permitting, at 11.00am, 2.30pm, and 7.00pm. Also at the peak of the holiday season during July and August, if it was a warm night, they would give what they termed a "Midnight Show". This was supposed to last from 10.30pm to 11.30pm, but often went on until midnight.    .

They did not repeat the same show *ad nauseam*, but had several changes of material during the season. For the daytime shows they wore the traditional pom pom and ruffled suits, but always appeared in evening dress for the late shows.

The portion of the Redcar pier which had survived was on the sea front opposite the end of Station Road. A glass shelter had been erected over the one-time skating rink and this became known as Cosy Corner. Billy ran his

18

*Billy Scarrow's Optimists of 1936. Billy Scarrow is standing second from right. The two deck chair boys sitting at the front of stage, left, both lost their lives in the Second World War. Their father is seated to the right.*

shows here for a number of years until in 1928 the "Glasshouse" as it was affectionately known was rebuilt as a theatre named the New Pavilion, which could seat in the region of eight hundred people.

Towards the end of the holiday season, usually late August into early September, Benefit Concerts were held. As was the practice with all seaside performers, the proceeds went to the performer who had been named for that particular evening. The performer often received tokens or gifts from delighted patrons in addition to his benefit money. The benefits were eagerly anticipated, as extra artists were often brought in, and the standard of entertainment was extremely high.

A popular feature promoted by the Optimists was a Local Talent Night, when anyone could take the stage and "do a turn". Prizes were awarded and the audience were the judges. Another feature of Billy's shows, which appears to have been exclusive to him, was the Lucky Numbers run by *Mr. Answers*. A magazine was sold amongst the audience at each performance for a few coppers. Each magazine was numbered and during the course of the show the winning numbers were drawn out of a hat. Mrs V. Alexander of Redcar tells us that the prizes were quite good and she still owns a cookery book and a set of Apostle spoons won at a Moonlight Show.

Because of the time span of Billy's shows it is obvious that the personnel changed many times over the years. Two performers, now well known to the viewing public, appeared with the Optimists in the 1930's. Billy Burden, the Dorset comedian who appeared on the Harry Worth television show, and more recently as a pig farmer in the "Hi de Hi" holiday camp series, was at Redcar for a few years just prior to the outbreak of war in 1939. The 1936 show included a

19

violinist called Jack le White. This gentleman, now quite elderly, has appeared recently in a television commercial for a well known insurance company. The two boys sitting on the edge of the stage in the picture of the 1936 company along with their father were the deck chair boys. Tragically, both were killed during the war.

There is a lovely story about two members of the company in Coronation year (1937). The drummer Len Woodland and the lady standing next to him in the Coronation group, Iris Hillier, fell in love. They married at Guisborough Registry Office in the morning, had a wedding breakfast and then returned to Redcar in time for the matinee and evening show. By this time their secret had spread around town and they were greeted by huge crowds of enthusiastic well wishers, and were showered with gifts.

To celebrate the Coronation of George VI an outing in the form of a rail excursion to Whitby was arranged but the prospect was a gloomy one. On the chosen day rain poured from leaden skies but obviously at this late hour it was not possible to rearrange the outing. As an alternative to indefinite postponement it was suggested that Billy Scarrow and the Optimists should be asked to join the outing, and so the pierrots travelled to Whitby with the old people. The Whitby Urban Council most obligingly placed the Spa Hall at the disposal of the party, and what could have been a bitter disappointment for all concerned became a memorable outing.

In the late 1930's when war was imminent, Billy's health began to deteriorate, though technically he still retained control. The high quality of the performances was maintained due to the respect and concern shown to him by his loyal troupe.

The outbreak of war in 1939 curtailed the season as people were apprehensive in the weeks leading up to the official declaration, and were not in the mood for holidays. This had an adverse effect on Billy's finances and unfortunately an altercation ensued with the local Council concerning the amount of money which should be paid for the pitch. This was eventually settled amicably, but that fateful year saw the last of what had become a local institution. Scarrow's Pierrots were no more. The demise of Billy took place in the early years of the war and he was buried in the town where he had spent so many happy years. His grave is in Redcar Lane Cemetery.

During the Second World War, in the early 1940's, Mr. Jack Videan, the proprietor of a grocer's shop in Marske High Street, organised a concert party with the admirable idea of entertaining the troops at Marske. The troupe was dressed in pierrot costumes and each wore a Yorkshire Rose badge.

Jack himself was the comedian and Mike Scott, a local teacher, was the straight man. Mathew Carter and his son Kit from Redcar did a turn. G. Pallant Sidaway entertained by drawing lightning sketches at the same time as he delivered jokes, much to the delight of the audience. The ladies of the cast were Jack Videan's wife and Yvonne Sidaway, sister of the aforementioned. These people were not professional entertainers, but we feel that their praiseworthy efforts should not go unrecorded. There can be no doubt that they were greatly appreciated during those dark days.

After the War, when the men began to be demobilised, people once more

CORONATION OPTIMISTS

*Billy Scarrow's
Coronation Optimists.
Standing third and fourth
left are Iris Hillier and
Len Woodland who
married during this
season.*

*Len and Iris Woodland,
Billy Scarrow's Optimists,
1936.*

21

resumed the practice of taking seaside holidays. In 1946 Barry Wood brought a show to Redcar's New Pavilion. The show was entitled "Radio Tymes". The star was a talented female impersonator called Billy Breen. He was the envy of the local girls with his fabulous dresses and much coveted nylon stockings. The show was a great success, but it is doubtful if anyone during this period imagined that he would reach the heights which he has now attained. Billy changed his act and his name. We now know him as Larry Grayson.

At this period a Redcar man by the name of Alan Gale was demobilised and returned to his native town. Alan was born in Redcar in 1916. In 1925 at the age of nine he appeared on the stage at Will Jowsey's Arcadia Theatre in Wilton Street, having enthusiastically volunteered nightly to assist the star of the show in his experiments. The star in question was the great Doctor Walford Bodie, whose act of "Electrical Wizardry" was famous in the Halls. He left school at the age of fourteen and by this time, nurtured by his nightly performance five years earlier, he was obsessed by the ambition of a stage career. He took a job as a bell boy at the Metropole Hotel in Whitby, but his heart was not in the job. His chance came when Teddy Joyce's Junior Dance Band was booked to appear at the Pier Ballroom in Redcar. For some reason they had been let down by their trumpet player. Alan who could play both trumpet and accordian, seized the opportunity, and was invited to tour with them.

After the tour ended, he was fortunate enough to have the chance to join Jimmy Slater's Super Follies at Cleethorpes. He was extremely versatile and in addition to his own musical act he obliged as feed for Freddie Frinton, the Grimsby born comedian who appeared with the Follies for five seasons. Alan next joined Ernie Moss's Sea Farers at Blackpool in the mid 1930's and stayed with them until 1939 when like many other performers he went to war having joined the Merchant Navy.

After demobilisation in 1946, he tendered for a site on Redcar beach. The fee for the site was £120. Alan invested his gratuity and a lot of hard work in an alfresco, and once more the pierrots were back on Redcar beach. The show opened on Victory Day, June 8th, and ran for a thirteen week season which ended in September. Assisted by his wife Pat Riding, who was an extremely versatile performer, he produced, performed in, and ran the shows. There was always a children's competition, which like those of the pre-war days, proved extremely popular. Alan is fondly remembered by older residents of Redcar for his rendition of *There's a Hole In My Bucket*. This was a favourite with him and was apparently performed with predictable regularity.

The troupe consisted of Alan and four other men who wore satin pierrot suits and skull caps, and four female members who wore satin dresses with frills at the neck. The pianist was Jan Paon, Wilson Leslie was a fine baritone, Billy Newman was the comedian and Harry Tracey was a female impersonator. The ladies were: Pat Riding, an extremely versatile entertainer; Ethel Formby, the sister of young George Formby, did songs to her own accompaniment on the ukelele, and was also a comedienne; Terri Morton, a clever dancer; and to complete the company a soubrette called Phyllis Bebe. Alan himself was an all round entertainer, doing instrumental turns, acting in the sketches, contributing the occasional comic song, indeed anything else amusing he could think up.

22

*The young Alan Gale.*

*Alan Gale's Wavelets,
1948, with Alan (centre) in
evening suit. Pictured
bottom left are Pat Riding
(Mrs Gale) and Ethel
Formby (sister of George
Formby).*

The show ended when Alan went to London in 1951. He claimed to have been concerned with the last pierrot troupe to appear on the beach. He now specialised in novelty presentations such as Lester's Midgets. These midgets had small houses specially designed for them, which were eventually passed on to a children's home in Kent by Alan. By this time he had become extremely interested in Old Tyme Music Hall and in 1953 he staged his first production at Hornsea, and eventually produced shows at various south coast venues. These were surely the fore-runners of the television series "The Good Old Days".

In 1972 Alan staged a show in Scarborough at the Grand Hotel and later at the Castle Hotel. He had a Jolson act, performances of which were extremely popular, and a number called *Pierrot Parade* in memory of the famous men who came to Scarborough in the 1890's and began it all. He stayed with his show in Scarborough until 1980.

Alan died at his home in Bromley on November 3rd 1986, aged seventy. He had, the previous summer, produced a show at the Cliftonville Lido from home as he was not well enough to work in the normal way. He had a daughter Julia who is an actress, and his son is now well known to television viewers as Peter Duncan, from such shows as Blue Peter and Duncan Dares. Peter has also acquitted himself creditably in Pantomime, and appears to be continuing the family tradition.

Since Alan Gale, the tradition of entertainment in Redcar has continued, but the concept is different from the old style pierrot shows and traditions.

# SALTBURN

Saltburn, like its near neighbour Redcar, was much favoured by the inhabitants of the industrial towns and cities of the north. It was widely renowned for its clean, bracing air, which must surely have been a great attraction to those who were daily accustomed to the grime and dirt generated by industry. Every advantage had been taken of a charming wooded glen, which was tastefully landscaped with gardens affording a peaceful retreat for those who wished to enjoy such a facility.

The firm, sandy beach stretched to the mouth of the Tees and there were approximately eight miles of golden sands, which were ideal for the stage and later the alfresco of the pierrots, and the ubiquitous bathing machines of the late Victorian and Edwardian period.

It had been decided that Saltburn should make every attempt to attract its fair share of visitors, and with this aim in mind a pier was built in the years 1868-70. Like other piers along this part of the coast it suffered the ravages of the storms during the winter of 1874-75. In 1900 the damaged portion was removed, thus reducing its length. The remaining part of the pier was refurbished. This proved to be an excellent decision as it once again attained immense popularity as a feature of the resort. During inclement weather, it provided shelter on innumerable occasions for the gallant pierrots who undeterred performed "under the pier if wet".

In 1925 a theatre was built on the pier which proved an added attraction and a band was usually engaged for the season. There was a diversity of street entertainers in the nineteenth century mainly of the circus type, acrobats, jugglers and performing animals. Another popular feature was the firework display which marked the annual opening of the Pleasure Gardens for the holiday season. Saltburn offered excellent accommodation for the holidaymakers in the form of long streets of large, well-built stone houses some of which were rented to visitors for varying periods of time; others were comfortable boarding houses which catered for the less affluent families who came only for a week in the summer.

One of the earliest troupes of seaside entertainers on the sands at Saltburn was Little Tommy's "Nigger Troupe" who performed near the cliff lift. They were of course black face minstrels. There was also in the early 1890's Mulvana's Minstrels of Whitby origin. Bert Grapho, Billy Jackson and Phil Rees, all of whom were to return as pierrots, appeared with Joe Mulvana.

John Middleton is credited with presenting the first pierrot troupe on the sands at Saltburn, but he soon sold out to Bert Grapho. Bert and Hamilton (Billy) Jackson had toured the Halls as a comedy act for some years and in 1894 they decided to speculate as promoters of a concert party, giving their first show at the Winter Gardens in Abingdon Park, Northants.

It was in the summer of 1899 that Saltburn visitors were first entertained by Grapho and Jackson's Jovial Jollies. This was to be the beginning of a forty year association with the town which continued through the First World War but was sadly ended in 1939 by the outbreak of another war.

The original troupe had the three members who had been together with Joe Mulvana: Bert who was a comedian and did a speciality act producing lightning cartoons; Billy Jackson as pianist; and Phil Rees known affectionately as "Little Phil". Phil's voice was as yet unbroken and the boy soprano brought tears to many an eye with his rendition of *The Blind Boy*. Phil was to form his own troupe at a later date called The Stable Boys, which included the now famous Jimmy James, at that period billed as Terry Casey "the Blue Eyed Boy". There was also in Bert's original troupe a harpist called Billy Brooks.

Grapho and Jackson were partners until 1911 when Jackson formed his own concert party and Bert continued with the Jovial Jollies ably assisted by his wife and later his adopted son, young Jack. It was during a winter season in Dumbarton that Bert and his wife decided to adopt young Jack McAlpine who at nine years old was already a very able performer. Bert determined to put on a show in the Halls, featuring young Jack, which he called "What a Lad" touring for some years.

The Jovial Jollies, in the early days, had only the boards laid on the sands on which to perform, but eventually they had an alfresco on the lower promenade. There were deck chairs for the patrons, and forms for the children placed directly in front of the stage. The price of a seat in this privileged position was one penny. There was a large iron shelter opposite the alfresco which was usually well filled by the early arrivals. This was so placed that the fortunate had what could be described as a dress circle seat and on Benefit Nights a real scramble ensued for this coveted position.

Like the performers in other towns, the Jovial Jollies were charged a fee for the pitch. The town records show that in 1901 they paid a fee of £10 for the season, but as in other places, when the Council realised their potential the fee began to rise. By 1906 it had risen to £50. There is no doubt that as the years passed the troupes were asked for ever increasing amounts. In the early days, there were no changing facilities and two bathing tents were used as "dressing rooms". These appear to have been a source of fascination to many of the children, who having temporarily escaped parental control poked their heads through the flaps to spy on the pierrots thus depriving them of what little privacy they had.

Eventually the Council agreed that the troupe should, during the month of August, the peak of the holiday season, give their evening shows in the Bandstand in Hazel Grove Gardens. Fairy lights were strung up in the trees to add to the carnival atmosphere which pervaded these special shows on the warm summer evenings. There is no doubt that many people carried away happy memories which were to remain with them for the rest of their lives.

Over the years the company changed several times, more members were added and other venues were explored but the Jollies always came back to Saltburn for the summer even though Bert now had alternative troupes performing in other venues.

*Grapho and Jackson's early Company, 1905.*

*Bert Grapho's Jovial Jollies. Top row (left), "Tag", Bert Grapho. Second row, far right, Tony Spoors. Bottom centre, Jack Grapho.*

In the 1906 summer season a Scottish comedienne called Mary Martin joined the troupe. This was an event which had far reaching ramifications for the Grapho family as Mary stayed with them in the capacity of performer, wardrobe mistress, family friend and eventually in the latter years of "Mrs Bert's" life, manager of the troupe and constant companion. Bert also had a son "Young Bert" who was a female impersonator, and was married to a lady known as Dolly Dubarry. Young Bert had his own troupe, but never appeared at Saltburn, their regular venue being at Cleveleys near Blackpool.

At the beginning of May 1929, Bert who had been in indifferent health for some time, died after a seizure. He was taken to Liverpool where he had made his permanent home but never recovered consciousness. In the true tradition Bert's wife, whose maiden name was Eliza Emma Pimlott, decided to carry on at Saltburn ably assisted by Jack. Although a native of Liverpool, she had over the years become very much involved with the Jovial Jollies and Saltburn. Mrs Bert, as she was affectionately known, was a small woman, but what she lacked in stature she is said to have gained in courage and determination.

Jean Atkinson who was a dancer with the Jovial Jollies at this period remembers how courageous she was when Bert died, and received a great deal of respect and affection from the members of the troupe, and also from people in official positions with whom she negotiated on business levels. She was also a very familar figure to the townspeople of Saltburn who regarded her with affection.

After Bert's untimely death, Jack took over as leading comedian with Ernie Miller as feed. Jack's catchphrase was "Eh, if ivver a man suffered". Like the rest of the family, Jack was very popular locally. He was, as were many of the men who performed with the pierrot troupes, extremely fond of children, giving encouragement to many a timorous youngster who rashly entered the talent contest, and was then struck dumb by stage fright. He was horrified on one occasion when he saw a child straying onto the rails of the cliff lift, in the track of a descending car. With complete disregard for his own safety he leapt over the fence and snatched the astonished child from certain death as the car drew closer. In recognition of his bravery he was presented with a suitably engraved gold watch by the townspeople.

In the 1930's when Jack took over the troupe the male members of the company wore black costumes with orange pom poms. The ladies wore black stockings but Jean Atkinson, who had trained as a classical dancer, found it impossible to dance in the stockings, so she was allowed bare legs and ballet shoes. They wore the pierrot outfits for the first half of the show, but clothes appropriate to the acts for the second half. Jean's partner at this period in duo acts was Marjorie Chapman.

Tony Spoors remained with the troupe for many years and was regarded in his capacity of resident pianist, as somewhat of a fixture. Another such was La Tagarte, known to the visitors as "Larty Garty" and to his fellow artistes as "Tag". His full name was William Tagarte Craugon. He had a remarkable baritone voice and was always billed as the Italian Baritone. It was said that he had once sung at "La Scala" in Milan, but this may be apocryphal. On Benefit Nights he astonished and delighted the audiences by dressing as a female Prima

*Grapho's Troupe c. 1930. From left to right: Ernie Miller, Jack Carlton, Sadie Pascall, Eva Walker, Mae Johns, Jean Atkinson, Tony Spoors, La Tagarte and Jack Grapho.*

Donna and declaiming in a shrill, high pitched falsetto voice. During the Second World War, Tag, who was past conscription age, worked at the rope works in Thornaby, and sang in the working men's clubs providing his own accompaniment on the piano.

Jean Atkinson originally appeared with the troupe full-time, but after her marriage in 1933, she worked "when needed" which appears to have been very often. She was with them when they gave their final performance in the September of 1939, a few days after the declaration of war.

In the middle of the performance the air raid siren sounded. The audience immediately fled in the direction of the shelters and the pierrots realised they were playing to empty benches. They were naturally very disappointed that the Germans had spoiled their last show. Ironically no bombs were dropped on that occasion as no enemy aircraft appeared, but the bewildered public responded to the recently published instructions for such emergencies.

In the halcyon days of the thirties, after the lean days of unemployment in the twenties, times slowly became more prosperous in the years which led up to the war. Holidays for the working classes were now a reality instead of a dream. During this period the pierrots in their usual manner worked extremely hard at their three shows a day in accordance with tides and weather. They lived in a large house on the Top Promenade, and the high spot of the day for many a child was to accompany the pierrots either up or down the winding path between performances.

The outbreak of the Second World War saw the end of the pierrots in Saltburn, and unfortunately many other towns. Post war audiences demanded more sophistication in shows, the merits of which are often debatable.

Mrs Bert lived on in Saltburn until her death on the 13th of September 1954, at the age of eighty four. After her death, young Jack, as he was still known, in spite of the fact that he was now middle-aged, went to London where he reverted to his original name of McAlpine. He was a real trouper and in spite of his chronic ill health continued to perform until he died in 1970.

# WHITBY

Whitby is a fishing port, its history dating back to the Celtic tribes who occupied Britain before the arrival of the Romans.

The town is tucked away in the cliffs at the mouth of the river Esk, built on both sides of the river, the houses rising steeply above the harbour. It has a quaint charm which appeals to many people. Its admirable situation between the Tyne and the Humber, and its proximity to the beautiful North Yorkshire moors has assured its popularity as a health resort. In 1848 development began in the West Cliff area to provide accommodation for visitors, and the "Khyber Pass" was cut to provide a path between West Cliff and the Pier. The Spa Theatre was built by Sir George Elliot, and musical and dramatic performances were given in the theatre. The pierrots were a popular form of entertainment on the foreshore in favourable weather.

Whitby was primarily a fishing town, but it had another rather unusual industry for which it is now widely known. Remunerative employment could be found in the manufacture of jet ornaments. A jet worker by the name of John Carlill was producing ornamental pieces as early as 1598, but the industry gained impetus during the mid nineteenth century. Jet was introduced into Queen Victoria's Court during a period of mourning and this brought even more prosperity to the town. The jet workers of this period earned exceptional wages and the town flourished.

In 1880 Sir George Elliot decided to give the town a centre for the enjoyment of visitors and residents alike. The Spa Pavilion and Colonnade Promenade were built on West Cliff. The Spa was surrounded by sunken gardens, putting greens and such. There were a theatre, reading rooms, refreshment room; and an orchestra played on the promenade twice daily during the summer months, while the visitors enjoyed the coastal panorama which could be viewed. A cannon from the Crimea was positioned near the entrance to the grounds.

The Spa was purchased from the Trustees of the West Cliff Estate by Whitby Urban District Council in 1915. This theatre became the venue for the concert parties who in the early days had often appeared on the sands.

Whitby was initially somewhat isolated but in 1836 the Whitby Pickering Railway was completed, and in 1883 the coast line to Scarborough and Saltburn was opened. Visitors were quick to take advantage of the many attractive amenities, thus adding to the prosperity of this rapidly expanding town. Unfortunately this prosperity was short-lived. The jet industry suffered a decline in trade due to the capricious whims of fashion, and unemployment became a problem. Fortunately the visitors had discovered Whitby and it did retain its popularity.

Possibly the earliest concert party on the beach at Whitby began as a result of the decline of the jet trade. Joe Mulvana was a jet turner in Whitby. Brooches, ear rings, necklaces and all manner of bijouterie were very popular amongst the ladies of the Victorian period. Joe was one of the craftsmen who lost his job following the decline of the jet trade, and cast around urgently to find employment in order to keep his wife and nine children. He tried several manual jobs none of which appealed to him.

When he was young, Joe's mother had earned a few shillings to augment the family income as a wardrobe mistress at the theatre. Young Joe was often taken to the theatre with his mother, possibly because it was the most convenient way of keeping her eye on him. This early experience, no doubt had some influence on him when he decided to form a minstrel troupe. His son Harry Mulvana played the banjo and could tap dance to some extent. Joe wore a top hat and cut-away coat with silk lapels and sported a large floral buttonhole. He did not "black up" but the rest of the troupe which consisted of seven men performed in black face and wore straw hats, light coloured trousers, and loose fitting tops with sailor collars.

The black face was achieved by the use of burnt cork. This appears to have been a somewhat messy business. A pile of corks was set alight and when burnt immersed in water until waterlogged. They were then squeezed and the resulting muddy residue conserved; when applied to the face it dried quickly giving a nice finish. It has been said that perhaps the most famous of black-faced entertainers, G.H. Elliott, used only champagne corks.

Joe first appeared in Whitby about 1880 and performed there for several years. He was possibly the first minstrel show on the Yorkshire coast although Christie's had begun several years earlier at Southport on the west coast. Bert Grapho and Billy Jackson who were later to form the Saltburn company in their own names both appeared with Mulvana's minstrels.

Possibly due to its proximity to Scarborough, Will Catlin who had successfully established himself in that town, decided to try a pierrot troupe at Whitby. By 1903 the Royal Pierrots under the management of Kennedy Scott were performing on the West Cliff. The troupe also included Ernest Hampton as pianist, Steve Roberts, Chas Arnett and Will Bradley. This appears to have caused some consternation amongst the middle class inhabitants of the area many of whom came to Whitby year after year. Complaints were registered in the appropriate quarters and the pierrots were duly banished once more to the beach.

George Royle came to Whitby in the summer of 1907. He had appeared in Blackpool for a few seasons with a troupe which he called the "Troubadours" but they were not very successful so he decided to take his show to the east coast. The move proved to be lucrative for George. He changed the name of the troupe to the Imps which was a shortened form of Imperials. He dressed them in stockings and knee breeches; they wore tunics with pointed collars and cuffs and pom pom trimmings and belts with pouches. The ladies' costumes were complementary. They played on the sands in fine weather but on rainy days took advantage of Lindsay Edward's Waterloo Hall on Flowergate. Benefits were always held in the hall. The original company included Gus Davis, Mark (Scottie) Daly, who was later to find fame on the West End stage, Sybil Glynne

*George Royle's Imps.*

and Lora Lyndon.

George Royal was born in 1877 and was always an entertainer. After Whitby he took his Imps to Scarborough where they were to become the famous "Fol-de-Rols."

In the years of the Second World War George went to South Africa with ENSA and at the cessation of hostilities he and his wife joined their son in Wellington, New Zealand. There they had nine happy years before George died on the 28th December 1957 at the age of eighty. Mrs Royle did not long outlive her husband; she died five days later on the 2nd January 1958.

In the season of 1911, Edward Allnutt and his Gay Cadets came to Whitby and appeared for four seasons until the outbreak of war. They favoured the blazers and yachting caps, popular at the time. Their morning performances on the beach began at 11.15am depending on the tide and the afternoon and evening shows at 3.15pm and 7.45pm respectively on Battery Parade. They also performed in the traditional pierrot costumes on occasion. Ted Allnutt later became the manager of the Empire Cinema at Whitby.

Leslie Fuller's Pedlars concert party appeared at the Coliseum in Whitby from 1910 to 1914. The Fuller brothers Leslie and Dave were both associated with concert parties, Leslie at one time being very popular on the south coast round the Margate area. During the First World War, Dave produced forces' concert parties. The Pedlars returned to Whitby in 1919 under the direction of Lieutenant Leslie Fuller and became a summer institution appearing every season throughout the 1920's and into the 1930's.

Wilby Lunn produced shows at the Whitby Spa Theatre for many years. He had been in partnership with Murray Ashford sharing the direction of the Bouquets concert party. In the 1920's Wilby had an act going with Connie Hart.

The double act was based on marionettes, reproducing the jerky actions and movements of the dolls. Wilby eventually took sole control of the Bouquets and they were still appearing annually at the Spa for the summer season in the 1960's.

*Bertram Noel, one of George Royle's Imps, 1911.*

*E. Allnutt Junior's Gay Cadets, 1912.*

*Leslie Fuller's Pedlars Concert Party, 1919.*

*Murray Ashford's Bouquets.*

# SCARBOROUGH

Scarborough has two bays, North and South. North bay is divided from South bay by a promontory which is crowned by the ruins of an ancient castle. North bay is enclosed by high cliffs and has always been popular with the more mature visitors, being the quieter of the two beaches. Its close proximity to the delights of Peasholme Park and Glen recommend it to many people who enjoy the contrast. Around the turn of the century the pierrots were a popular feature on the beach in North bay.

South bay has the harbour and fish quay. The unloading of the catch has been a focal point of interest for many years with visitors. The Old Town is situated above the harbour. The Spa is an attractive asset to the bay, having over the years provided a venue for many types of entertainment. It was originally the source of medicinal waters.

It was the discovery of these waters that brought fame to Scarborough as a resort. The spring was discovered in the rocks in South bay and in a very short time gentry and nobility began to frequent the town. Royal patronage in the mid 1700's assured its popularity.

Scarborough wisely began to provide amenities to cater for the visitors in the form of gaming tables, and billiards; bookshops combined with circulating libraries, where books could be borrowed for a small fee, prospered. Dancing and music were provided in the evenings. Interest in the Spa waters waned as the popularity of the amenities spread.

The sands in South bay are extremely fine and by the mid 1800's were well supplied with bathing machines and other attractions beloved by the Victorian and Edwardian visitors to the town. The area below the Spa was highly coveted as a pitch by the pierrots, the wall providing a certain amount of free seating for the audiences. There was a growing interest in various forms of the theatre and a diversity of entertainments was offered.

The visitors were now swarming to Scarborough on the excursion trains provided, arriving at the town with alarming regularity at very short intervals.

Between the years 1866 and 1869, the North Pier was built, but in 1883 a ship collided with the pier causing serious damage. In 1889 the Pavilion was built. The pier was never really patronised in the manner it deserved. A few anglers availed themselves of this amenity, but the fault possibly lay in the fact that adequate access was not provided. The Marine Drive should have been constructed much earlier. The situation was finally resolved in January 1905, when the Pavilion and the remainder of the pier were literally blown away overnight in a terrible storm by gales of incredible velocity.

The beach on the South side which had once been a place for the decorous promenades of fashionable ladies, now became a place of fun and enjoyment.

It was in this atmosphere that the minstrels tested their fortunes along with the Punch and Judy shows, ice cream vendors, pedlars, fortune tellers and of course the ubiquitous donkeys, without which no beach was complete at this period. Occasional open air religious services were held. The pattern was well established by the time that Tom Carrick and Will Catlin came to Scarborough. Charles Laughton of Hollywood fame who was born in Scarborough is reputed to have been greatly attracted to the pierrots in his youth.

The resort has always been popular with folk from the heavy woollen district of the West Riding, where the pierrots performed during their winter tours. Visitors from Leeds and Bradford regularly sought out their favourites during the summer season.

The earliest regular seaside entertainers in Scarborough were the Home Minstrels. They performed in the late 1880's and early 1890's. Mostly amateurs, included in their ranks were David Hunter who played cricket for Yorkshire and was an excellent dancer; J.W.H. Catley, a popular local personality who acted as "Mr. Interlocutor"; and Quinton Gibson who had a most unusual alto voice and was acclaimed as a very accomplished female impersonator. He was in great demand in Yorkshire as a pantomime dame and appeared in various productions. The Home Minstrels performed for charity. Quinton Gibson, in partnership with Leo Dryden ran a troupe which performed on the North pier. Quinton was in charge of organising the entertainments programme for the ill-fated pier and is recorded as having presented the first concert in 1890, and the last in 1904.

Another early troupe to appear at Scarborough were Joe Mulvana's Minstrels already mentioned as regular performers at Whitby. Bert Grapho who began with Mulvana and later formed a troupe of pierrots at Saltburn, also did a season here prior to his establishment further north.

Josh Wells was another performer, hailing from Leicester. There were four men in his troupe, and on summer evenings they gave shows on South Cliff. They commenced in Prince of Wales Terrace and usually ended their shows for the public at around 10p.m outside the Crown Hotel. Joe played the concertina and his many admirers in Scarborough presented him with an instrument of which he was very proud.

Johnny Groves was performing in Scarborough at an early date. He was a local man and employed local artists wherever possible. As previously mentioned, he later moved to Redcar. His pitch was on the sands in front of what is now the Futurist Theatre, and when the tide was too high, on the Esplanade and Queens Parade on North cliff. His show was often interrupted by the traffic on the road which passed between the performers and the audience. Minor setbacks of this nature were not allowed to interfere with the show.

During the 1880's, when the minstrels were entertaining the residents and holidaymakers on the beaches and streets of Scarborough, permits were required to perform in the town. The police were responsible for the issue of these, and the performer in charge of a troupe was expected to present himself each Monday morning at the police station and pay the sum of one shilling (5p) per artist, or as in popular phraseology, "a bob a nob a week".

The first actual pierrot troupe to appear on the beach at Scarborough was Sidney James's Strolling Players. They consisted of Claude West, Molly Sey-

*Carrick's Popular Pierrots, 1904 (Carrick, standing).*

mour who accompanied them on the strill, and a young man by the name of Tom Carrick.

Tom Carrick was astute enough to realise the potential of this kind of entertainment, and by the early 1890's had formed his own group. This initially consisted of himself, Gus and Claude West, and Sidney James. Carrick was an extremely likeable character. He had a quirky, clown like, smiling face, and always spoke in a broad northern accent which enhanced his performance of comic songs, delivered at breakneck speed. A typical example ran thus:

> *He knew all about etymology,*
> *Hebrew, Shebrew and phrenology,*
> *Syntax, tin tax, hob nailed boot jacks*
> *etc. etc.*

He always tried to involve his audience in these tongue twisting, jaw breaking exercises. His ploy was to start at a normal speed and increase the speed leaving his audience laughing and gasping for breath. The boys were all dressed in the traditional white suits with red pom poms. Renowned for his generosity, Carrick had a heart of pure gold. Never making much in the way of profit for himself, he was always willing to lend a helping hand to his performers, many of whom made the grade with their own shows.

Sidney Leighton, and a lady pianist Bessie James were added to the troupe, and in 1906 when Will Catlin bought the sole rights for performing on the sands, Carrick took his show to the open air skating rink on the roof of the Grand Restaurant. He also played at the Floral Pavilion with a troupe which he called Carrick's White Musketeers.

*Carrick's Popular Pierrots, 1905.*

40

*Carrick's Alfresco on Scarborough Sands, 1903.*

*Catlin's Favourite Pierrots, South Shore, 1905.*

41

*Will Catlin, founder of the famous Pierrot Troupe.*

William Henry Fox was born in Leicester in 1871. His father, a publican, was the landlord of the King William IV in Colton Street, and was also a county cricketer of some distinction.

Young Will was educated at the British Boys School, and in due course was apprenticed to a tailor's cutter. This was not entirely to his liking and it was very soon obvious that he had no intention of staying in such a mundane occupation, although the little experience he gained was to prove most useful at a later date.

He had been interested in the stage from a very early age, and as an adolescent became a familiar figure on the concert platforms around Leicester. He had a flair for entertainment and rapidly established a reputation as a polished amateur performer.

At the age of nineteen, undeterred by the fickleness of public taste and all the other hazards of earning one's living "on the boards", Will abandoned the occupation which did not appeal to him in favour of a professional career as an entertainer, producer and proprietor. Perhaps, it may be argued he was more fortunate than some, but nearer the truth is the fact that Will always made the most of every chance, and was never afraid of hard work. His first professional venture was with a young man called Charlie Carson (later Danton) as a double act on the music hall stage. It was at this juncture that he changed his name to Catlin. He simply decided that the double billing as Catlin and Carson was preferable to Fox and Carson. They worked in the Moss Stoll Syndicate and appeared in various parts of the country.

It was not until 1894 that Will Catlin first appeared in Scarborough. At this period entertainers were expected to work in any capacity, and Will formed a troupe who entertained on the sands. The following year he was engaged to appear at the Aquarium which was known as the People's Palace Music Hall under the direction of William Morgan. At this time he also appeared at the opening performance at the People's Palace in Bridlington.

The following year saw him back on the sands, and having spent a season in partnership, he took over the whole show. This was a step which was to influence the course of his life. His name was to become irrevocably linked with seaside entertainment and Scarborough. From a comparatively unknown performer he was to become one of the greatest pioneers of seaside entertainment in all its forms.

Catlin dressed his troupe in pierrot costumes consisting of black skull caps surmounted by a white conical hat, white suit with ruffles at neck and wrist and black pom poms. This garb was to become familiar to the seaside going public in later years, but in the 1890's was something of a novelty. From this modest beginning he was to establish a national reputation.

Will's brother Tom, sometimes referred to as Tom Braham-Fox, soon joined him in his venture, and there were two troupes running simultaneously, Will on South beach opposite the Aquarium and Tom's "Red Pom Poms" at North bay. Eventually he had troupes under his direction performing in numerous principal seaside resorts as far apart as Bournemouth and Whitley Bay. It became a tradition that one of his companies should appear at Bridlington for four or five weeks between Easter and Whitsuntide. Another Yorkshire venue

*Bert Lytton of Catlin's Pierrots.*

*Willie Manders, female impersonator.*

*Will Ambro, Pierrot and Director.*

*Sid Frere, jovial tenor.*

was Withernsea of which more will be recounted in the relevant chapter. Throughout all this expansion Will retained his interest in the Scarborough troupe.

The Catlin pierrot troupes were in the early years all male shows. It was not until the advent of the First World War and with it the subsequent shortage of male performers, which caused him, reluctantly, to engage female entertainers. It has been suggested that his aversion to women performers was possibly due to the fact that he had a family of one son and six daughters whom he openly discouraged from entering the profession. He forbade his children to marry into "the business" but in spite of this, two of his daughters, Gladys and Topsy, did eventually marry pierrots.

Catlin had very strict rules for his company, and was very astute in presenting his "boys" as desirable bachelors, so causing many female hearts to flutter and ensuring a devoted following. The pierrots were given strict instructions that they must never be seen walking arm in arm with a lady, even though some of them had wives. This image of availability was a very cunning and successful psychological ploy.

He was also shrewd enough to realise that instead of engaging performers for a few weeks in the summer, as most of his rivals did, he could offer permanent year round employment, thus securing the services of the finest performers in the business. This was achieved by touring his troupe around the inland towns and cities during the winter months. They regularly appeared at places such as Leeds, Bradford, Hull, Manchester, indeed anywhere that people needed entertaining with halls and theatres available.

This not only ensured him of the loyalty of his troupe, but also helped to advertise them for the forthcoming summer season, as many of the patrons of the winter shows were among the prospective holidaymakers, many of whom patronised Bridlington and Scarborough for their annual holidays.

The Catlin troupes were always immaculately dressed. Will now put to good use his brief experience of the tailoring trade. He designed and cut the costumes, and with the able assistance of his wife and daughters, produced the finished garments to a very high standard. It was noticeable, even in the early days, that his costumes were a much better fit and far superior to those of his rivals.

As previously mentioned Tom Carrick was already established in Scarborough when Will Catlin arrived in town. There was obviously rivalry between the two men for prime pitches on the beach which were auctioned by the Corporation each season. In 1906, Will cleverly secured all the pitches causing his rivals to move on to other venues. The original "rent" charged by the Corporation was still "a bob a nob" per day for each performer. This was six shillings (30p) per week per man, and amounted to a collective sum of five to six pounds per week.

The troupe gave three performances a day when the weather was fine. Only severe inclement weather or exceptionally high tides prevented them from entertaining. The money was collected from the people who paid for the deck chairs set out in front of the stage, and also by "bottling", passing a bag on the end of a stick amongst people standing on the wall or around the stage. The pierrots each took turns selling song sheets and copies of a publication called

*Catlin's Royal Pierrots. Catlin is pictured at the back in the dark costume.*

the Book of Songs, as sung by Catlin's Royal Pierrots. Early in the reign of Edward the Seventh Catlin's gave a Command Performance and changed their name from Catlin's Favourite Pierrots to Catlin's Royal Pierrots. The song book contained the words of fifty songs and could be purchased for the sum of twopence ($1\frac{1}{2}$p).

Another lucrative pursuit was the selling of picture postcards; these were available showing the whole troupe, or individual members each of whom had his own particular following amongst the spectators.

One of the early members of Will Catlin's initial troupe was Kemsley Scott Barrie. Born in Leeds he was a gifted comedian and female impersonator, and could turn his hand to almost any form of entertainment, including dancing and monologues. He was related to Sir Percy Scott, Admiral of the Fleet.

After some years with Catlin, he formed a troupe of his own which he called the Chanticleers. They initially appeared at the Harehills Pavilion in Leeds. The original group included another gifted performer who had appeared with Catlin's at Scarborough. His name was Will Ambro, an extremely accomplished comedian. In 1911 the Chanticleers moved to Undercliffe, Bradford and Scott Barrie engaged a local lad with a fine soprano voice, named Harry Mitchell. In 1912 Harry joined Will Catlin and stayed with the troupe until he went to war in 1915. The 1911 Troupe were attractively dressed in blue silk blouses and black knee breeches, the ladies dresses being complementary.

Scott Barrie was a very talented female impersonator appearing on many occasions in pantomime. In 1909 he took the part of Dame in the production of Alladin at the Lyceum Theatre in London. Another of his famous performances was as Mrs Desiccated Edwards, cook in Flockton Foster's production of Dick Whittington.

46

During the First World War, Scott Barrie was a leading member of the 62nd Divisional Concert Party known as the "Pelicans", from the regimental division sign. With his usual versatility he gave a good all round performance in shows behind the lines. In the early part of 1918, the Pelicans were given leave, and whilst in England performed at Leeds and Bradford. Apart from their shows all members of the troupe carried out normal military duties. It was whilst carrying out his duties as a stretcher bearer that Kemsley Scott Barrie received the wounds from which he later died. The irony is that he survived until the last few weeks before Armistice, dying on October 7th 1918 in France. He was buried at Le Treport, a sad loss to the world of entertainment.

Will Ambro, as already mentioned, was an early member of Will Catlin's Scarborough troupe, and appeared with them for a number of years. Not only was he a versatile performer but also a good producer. He was well known and respected among the patrons from the West Riding, and in 1906 along with Will Catlin, Tom Catlin, Scott Barrie and Bert Lytton, he went on the winter inland tour. In 1913, after a couple of seasons with the Chanticleers along with George Houghton, another Catlin man who became director of the Whitley Bay Troupe and also fell in France, he formed the "Debonairs". They appeared at the Kursaal in Marine Avenue, Whitley Bay. In the winter they brought the show to Shipley near Bradford, and added to the company a young Manxman by the name of Harry Korris.

Will Ambro appeared with numerous companies in the Yorkshire area over the years, and was well known in the county for his pantomime Dame performances. He produced two more season shows "The Criterions" and "New Superbs". It can be truthfully said that Will Ambro gave a lot of enjoyment to Yorkshire people.

It is impossible to write about the early days of the Catlin troupe without mentioning Willy Manders. He was born in Birmingham and christened William Henry Manders, one of a family of eleven. He was an enthusiastic amateur performer and delighted audiences in his native city on numerous occasions. It was at one of these shows that Will Catlin saw him, and was so impressed by his act that he signed him for a three year contract.

Whilst appearing with Catlin's Manders acquired a professional approach to production. It was during this period that he met and married his wife Gladys, who was Catlin's second daughter. Willie was very young, and the match did not meet with Will's approval, so the couple took advantage of her father's absence in Bridlington on business one day, and secretly married at Scarborough.

It was during his Birmingham days that Manders first donned the garb of a female impersonator. It came about because the company in which he was a member, was somewhat impecunious, and short of one gent's costume, so Willie wore a spare lady's outfit and proved an immediate success. This was to have far reaching results.

During the First World War, he served behind the lines as Sub-Lieutenant W.H. Manders with the 63rd Royal Naval Division. He was asked to take charge of a divisional Concert Party. They gave numerous shows behind the lines in France. Willie not only produced the shows, but appeared as a performer and became a big favourite with the Tommies. He did shows in France with

Leslie Henson and Eric Blore, a comedian who became famous for his potrayals of a butler in Hollywood musicals.

When Manders was demobilised, he formed 'The Quaintesques". For his first season he was booked at the Royal Princess Parade and Spa, Bridlington. His company in Catlin tradition was all male and consisted of seven members. The show was an immediate success. He went to Rhyl on a three day visit which resulted in him taking over the Pier Amphitheatre in 1921, where he remained until his death in 1950. He was deeply mourned, not only by local people but many others throughout the country to whom he had brought joy.

Sid Frere was a big jovial man with a mass of unruly auburn hair which he never successfully subdued. In spite of his efforts, strands always crept out from under his black skull cap. He was an accomplished performer with a fine sense of fun. He had a good tenor voice and he would sing a comic song amid gales of laughter, then follow it with a serious ballad superbly rendered. This ploy brought the house down and had the audiences clamouring for more. Sid, like many other pierrots, served his country during the First World War. Along with other Yorkshire pierrots he appeared with the famous Byng Boys. There is no doubt that this talented performer could have become a top of the bill headliner, but he loved the life of a pierrot and had no ambition to perform in any other context.

Harry Mitchell Craig, as previously stated, did not join Will Catlin until 1912. He then committed the cardinal sin (in Catlin's opinion) — he fell in love with Florence Catlin affectionately known as Topsy. She returned his love, but her father had forbidden his daughters to associate with pierrots and refused to give his consent to their marriage. Topsy eventually married a local jeweller with whom she lived happily for twenty five years until she was widowed. It was then that she discovered that Harry had never married. He had waited for her over the years and they now had twenty five years of happiness together until he died in 1970.

In 1920, when Harry was released from the forces he produced Ernest Binns' "Arcadians" in Bradford, then in 1924 he went to Rhyl and joined his old friend Willie Manders in his Quaintesques, remaining with him for several years as artist and producer. He went to Australia, then in the 1940's was manager and script-writer for Harry Korris during his Happidrame series with the B.B.C.. Harry ended his working days with the man who had influenced his life almost from the beginning of his career. He became director of productions at Catlin's Arcadia at Llandudno.

These are just a few of the personalities whom Catlin employed; there were many more of a similar calibre who helped him to success.

In the first year, Will's show on the beach made a modest profit, but as its popularity increased so did the demands of the Corporation for the rent of the pitches.

By 1903, they were demanding £650 and by 1908 the demands had become unreasonable, and were said to exceed four figures. Will's reaction to this situation was a flat refusal to pay. The councillors were mortified, but Catlin, not to be dismayed, moved the whole company to a new site near the Grand Hotel. The Council retaliated by declaring this unsafe so Catlin with his usual business acumen responded by buying some land where the present Futurist Theatre now stands, and erected a covered wooden alfresco for the shows. This was to become the first Arcadia Theatre. It was a complete wooden building with scope for producing more elaborate shows. It is estimated that during his years on the beach he built up his audiences and from a modest beginning with a very small profit, he consistently played to audiences of 2,000 seated patrons and as many standing. In the course of his career he made somewhere in the region of 20,000 personal appearances. It was at this period that he also acquired the rights to the Kiosk on Clarence Gardens. Due to the short sighted policy of the Council, the Corporation lost a lucrative contract. The Arcadia was the beginning of the foreshore developments which are synonymous with the name of Catlin.

Up to this time Will had lived in Leicester, but in 1910 he moved to Scarborough and took up permanent residence. He began a development programme which included the Arcadia Restaurant, the Palladium Cinema and the acquired Olympia. So perhaps it could be said that the Council did him a great favour.

Their next move was an attempt to curb his success by building a rival theatre. The Floral Hall was scheduled to open in 1910. This of course was much publicised. With his usual flair Catlin took the kind of action one had come to expect from this remarkable showman. He hired an expert balloonist by the name of Captain Spencer. He was to make an ascent from an area behind Catlin's theatre at a time calculated to lure prospective customers from the opening of the Floral Hall. The show was of course free, and with true Catlin efficiency it was equally well publicised. All he required was the one factor even he could not arrange, fine weather. Fate was obviously siding with him, for at the appropriate time for the balloon ascent the weather was perfect. Apart from the Council officials and friends, the Floral Hall was nearly empty.

In 1913, Will began an ambitious scheme which unfortunately was marred by the onset of hostilities a year later. The Kingscliffe Holiday Camp included a dining room capable of seating 520 people and a handsome concert hall with seating for 900 people. Sleeping and living facilities were intended to accommodate 1,000 people. He further endeared himself to the local population by employing only Scarborough men to do the work. A local contractor directed the work and a local architect prepared the plans.

At 8 o'clock on the morning of the 16th December 1914, the first attack on a British town by a foreign navy for more than a hundred years was made by six German warships. Their target was the coastal towns of the north east coast, Hartlepool, Whitby and Scarborough.

It had been a beautiful summer, ideal for seaside holidays with Catlin's Royal Pierrots performing on the south shore. At the outbreak of hostilities Scarborough began to take the usual defence precautions against invasion in the form of barbed wire barricades on all roads leading up from the cliffs, but no-one expected bombardment from the sea.

Will suffered a double blow as the holiday season was cut short when the excursion trains were discontinued to be used for the movement of troops and equipment. One of the first shells to land on Scarborough is said to have

49

*Catlin's Royal Pierrots at the Arcadia, 1913. Will Catlin, Louis Finch (pianist), Reg Dayre, Ernest Tilsbury, Clinton Carew, Frank A. Terry, Will Terry, Andrew McAllister, Billie Manders and Harry Mitchell-Craig.*

destroyed the show's entire wardrobe at Clarence Gardens, and damage was also caused at his Kingscliffe Camp.

One could be forgiven for assuming that the middle-aged Will would have rested on his laurels, having enjoyed so much success and adulation in his chosen profession. From modest beginnings he had performed before, and been presented to, Royalty, including Edward VII and the Prince of Wales, later to become King George V. He had turned down opportunities to perform on the London stage with staggering fees being offered and had become a man of property. This of course had not been achieved without a great deal of hard work and dedication. He did have a narrow escape with his life however. Whilst touring with the pantomime Robinson Crusoe, a wad of stage ammunition was embedded in his leg when a gun was discharged. This was before the advent of X rays, and over several days doctors made numerous attempts to dislodge the offending "bullet" by probing to no avail. This was a painful and traumatic experience, and it was feared that the limb might have to be amputated. Fortunately the wad was located and worked itself out. Undismayed Will was back on the boards as soon as he could stand.

Will never even considered retirement; for a short time the family moved back to Leicester, but were soon back in Scarborough. Whilst they were not allowed to perform the family had always been involved in his shows to the extent that the whole family always attended a new show and met afterwards to discuss it. This solid family background with its support helped Catlin through the years to reach the pinnacle of his success.

There were now Catlin shows in resorts too numerous to mention. He had always had a particular liking for the Welsh resort Llandudno. It was here that he chose to live out his later years. He never did retire, and was constantly to be seen at one or other of his theatres, taking a personal interest in the presentation of all his shows.

Two weeks before his death he made what was to be his last visit to Scarborough to see for himself the current show. His humorous and disheartening experiences made him a very understanding "guvnor". Never at any time did he ask one of his troupe to do anything he was not prepared to do himself. This was largely the key to his phenomenal success as it inspired confidence and support, coupled with his astute business acumen which motivated him to purchase one of the finest sites in Scarborough at the right time, and to make films of current events, including members of his troupes, thus putting them among the first of British film actors.

Catlin was advised to retire on more than one occasion, but the advice fell upon deaf ears. On the 15th January 1953 Will left his home in Llandudno with the object of seeing his show at the Arcadia Theatre. He was to have attended the rehearsal of Catlin's Follies, but he collapsed and died in his car outside the theatre at the age of eighty five. In true Catlin tradition the show went on that evening and the audience was not given the sad news until the end of the performance.

It could be said that Will Catlin was a big man in all senses of the word. He was tall, broad shouldered, and was said by those who knew him to have had an inspiring presence. An extremely astute businessman with a broad vision which marked him out as an exceptional person, he is often referred to as the "King of the Pierrots" a title which he justly deserved. It would be fair to say that he took the last exit in a way that if given choice, he would have chosen for himself. Showbusiness was his life and to the end of his very long career he was very much in charge down to the most trivial detail. To reach over eighty years and pass away still in harness, peacefully and without prolonged suffering is not given to most of us, but this end was surely deserved.

A conical pierrot hat made from white flowers rested on his coffin, bearing a card which read "King of the Pierrots final curtain, with deepest respect from 1953 Catlin's Follies". Surely a fitting tribute to a truly remarkable showman.

The first season at the Floral Hall in 1910 was played by "Cardow's Cadets", but was unremarkable.

In 1910 George Royle brought his "Imps" to Scarborough where they performed on the sands. He was approached by the Council to lease the newly constructed Floral Hall for the 1911 season.

This was a large metal and glass construction of a design much favoured at that period in many seaside resorts. The atmosphere created was reminiscent of the Edwardian conservatories. Hanging baskets with flowering plants were suspended from the ceiling, indoor rockeries were constructed, and artistic use was made of large parlour palms and the like.

Royle accepted the Council's offer but felt that the title Imps did not fit this salubrious environment. The mode of dress of the company was changed, the ladies wore crinolines, the men frock coats and toppers. The name was changed so as to be more in keeping with the metamorphosis — the "Fol-de-Rols" were born. George Royle took great care of his performers. He inspected their theatrical digs to ensure that they were suitable, and made random checks at

*Cardow's Cadets at the Floral Hall.*

*The Fol-De-Rols at the Floral Hall. Standing first and second from far right are Elsie and Doris Waters.*

intervals to ensure that the standards were maintained. He made a rule that his artists were not to associate with the beach performers; having come up in the world, he obviously intended staying there. Mrs Royle took charge of the wardrobe for the whole company.

On the opening night the star of the show was Dewey Gibson, a performer with a pleasing tenor voice who stole the show. Other members of the cast were Syd Hollister and Babs Du Cane, ably supported by their pianist Malcolm Ives. There were ten members in the original cast, and two programme changes per week. This ensured good attendances as holiday makers often returned after enjoying the first show. The Fols as they were affectionately known played at the Floral Hall until 1914. Like Catlin, Royle lost money when the season was curtailed by the outbreak of the First World War.

When he was offered the lease of the Floral Hall in 1918 on the cessation of hostilities, Royle was still very much aware of his earlier loss. The Council was also asking for a fee far in excess of their previous demand. He decided that it would be more prudent to share the risk by taking a partner. Greatrex Newman was introduced to him.

Born in Manchester in 1892, Newman began writing sketches and lyrics about 1914. His first efforts were used in "The Passing Show". During the War he served as a pilot in the Flying Corps.

It proved an ideal partnership as Newman had no interest in performing but enjoyed writing! Royle produced, Newman wrote and helped financially. Newman was associated with several shows between the wars including Joy Bells in 1919, a wartime show that transferred to the West End stage. He collaborated with Clifford Gray in the authorship of the popular Mr. Cinders, and contributed material to the programme of the famous Co-optimists under the direction of Davy Burnaby.

Over the years numerous people of note appeared with the Fols at Scarborough. Elsie and Doris Waters and Kathleen West, a superbly funny comedienne, were very popular.

In 1926 Newman took the Fols to Hastings where they proved a great success. They played there until the outbreak of war in 1939. Encouraged by the Hastings venture he produced Fols in numerous other resorts. George Royle retired in 1935, but Newman continued until 1960 when he sold out to Jack Hylton. During the Second World War Newman took companies to every war venue possible giving shows both on stage and from the backs of lorries. Many famous entertainers of the past began their careers with the Fols including Arthur Askey, Richard Murdoch, The Weston Brothers and Cyril Fletcher, to name but a few.

The north beach at Scarborough was frequented in the 1920's by "Feldman's Songsters". They were a troupe managed by Feldmans Music Publishers and sang only the songs published by the company. This gave them a very wide scope as Feldman produced many of the Music Hall songs of the day, including such classics as *"Yes We Have No Bananas"*.

Bert Feldman began his career in his father's music shop in Hull. He was given a copy of *"It's a Long Way to Tipperary"* by Jack Judge, the man who penned it. Bert possessed a lifelong uncanny talent for recognising a winning number, and this one made his fortune.

In 1925, George Horrocks presented an alfresco show "under the spa wall three times daily, tide and weather permitting". He called the troupe "The Radio's". The performers also participated in gala concerts given in Peasholme Park on Wednesday evenings. George Horrocks later became Borough Entertainments Officer.

These were the men and women who entertained Scarborough residents and visitors at the end of the nineteenth century and during the first decades of the present. Since this time Scarborough has had many notable shows and entertainments but these have become more sophisticated and are far removed from the conditions endured by those intrepid beach performers of the early days.

# FILEY

Filey, at the beginning of the nineteenth century was a fishing village. Filey bay lies between the Brigg and Bempton Cliffs. On the north side is a headland known as Carr Naze, from which the Brigg runs out into the sea for a considerable distance, providing a natural breakwater and affording some protection to the bay against storms. Bempton Cliffs are of course well known as a breeding ground for thousands of seabirds. This sheer wall of rock is an impressive sight, being estimated at about four hundred feet in height. Unlike most of the other Yorkshire coastal resorts, Filey never had a pier, and has no harbour. The fishermen launch their boats straight down the beach from the coble wharf.

In old Filey, there are still some houses of seventeenth century origin, one of which is reputed to have a connection with smugglers. St. Oswald's Church, where the grave of Andie Caine is to be found, is at the top of a beach road called the Ravine, which is like a tunnel formed by trees. The church is reached by an iron bridge which spans a road. When Charlotte Bronte stayed at Cliff House in Filey, she regularly attended St. Oswald's and wrote letters home about the church. The incumbent for many years was Canon Cooper, more widely known as the famous "Walking Parson".

Filey began to change in the 1830's, just prior to the accession to the throne of Queen Victoria. Several villas were built on the south cliff for the accommodation of visitors, and an extra amenitiy in the form of a bath house was built. People were gradually being attracted to Filey by the bracing air, which was declared to be very healthy and beneficial to those in less than robust condition.

When in 1847 Filey was linked by rail to Hull and York, it developed into an extremely pleasant resort much favoured by the upper middle classes, particularly the clergy and their families, and also high ranking Army and Navy officers. Royalty were attracted to Filey, Prince and Princess Louis of Battenberg visiting on more than one occasion. Such literary worthies as Edward Lear and Charlotte Bronte appear to have found it congenial.

The residential visitors were increasingly catered for and encouraged, either in the new hotels or as families who rented the same houses or villas season after season. Not surprisingly, some of these visitors took an interest in the fisher folk and lasting friendships were formed. This to some extent established the character of the town, as the tradition persisted over the years. Filey has never attracted the day trippers who in their hoardes flocked to its neighbours, Bridlington and Scarborough.

As early as 1857, Filey could boast a first class photographer by the name of Mr. Fisher. His services were eagerly sought to provide the "carte de visite" and later cabinet photographs which enhanced the large family albums so dear to the Victorians. High class grocers, drapers and provision merchants were much in evidence, who vied with each other to provide the type of service and range of goods to which the visitors were accustomed, and agreeably surprised to find in a small coastal resort.

This was the place with its fine stretch of firm sands that provided an ideal venue for the pierrots when they came to town around the turn of the twentieth century.

Andie Taylor was born in 1867. His parentage is unknown as Andie was raised in an orphanage, so perhaps there was personal tragedy early in his life, but this does not appear to have had any adverse effect upon his character. He later changed his name to Andie Caine, and became one of the best loved and respected citizens of Filey.

There is some doubt as to the actual date when Andie first entertained on Filey beach. Two schools of thought exist on this subject, but the concensus of opinion would suggest the summer of 1894. On more than one occasion Andie is reputed to have said that he made his way to Filey after a season or two with Will Catlin at both Scarborough and Bridlington.

If this is correct, and there are photographs to substantiate this claim, it would place his first appearances in Filey nearer to the turn of this century as Will Catlin began his career on the north east coast in 1896. It is possible that this confusion has arisen due to an earlier troupe of entertainers (whose name no-one remembers) and whose performances were short lived. There is also evidence to support the claim that Andie appeared with Chas. Beanland for a season in the mid-nineties on a pitch at Beaconsfield, which was later to become the bowling green in Bridlington.

Andie originally came to Filey as a busker along with George Fisher. They wore pierrot costumes; Andie played the banjo and delighted his audiences with

*Andie Caine's Troupe around the turn of the century.*

such favourites as *Just a Little Bit of String* and *Said the Bird on Nellie's Hat*, given out in a good strong tenor voice. George, whose instrument was the strill, or portable harmonium, which was by virtue of its mobility the mainstay of many a pierrot troupe, gave a stirring rendition of *Genevieve*.

They were soon joined by Teddy Myles, a comedian from Leeds who was to stay with Andie for several seasons. In spite of the fact that they "bottled" vigorously, they could not afford digs and slept on the sands. Andie was a man of some fortitude and not easily daunted. A story which has passed down the years orally claims that he walked from London, originally to join the East Coast Entertainers. No evidence can be found to substantiate this story (neither can it be disproved) but it was still being mentioned in entertainment circles in the late 1930's.

In the early days there was unfortunately some animosity between the local fishermen and the performers. The fishermen considered the pierrots a nuisance, and interfered with their working conditions. They tried to discourage them or at least move them on by dumping fish guts and other disgusting detritus on their pitch. This naturally fostered resentment, but a timely word from the local police sergeant seems to have de-fused what was developing into an ugly situation. The fishermen began to realise, no doubt after this was pointed out to them, that the entertainers were attracting people to the resort, which of course opened up the promise of more trade for them, and the practices ceased.

Once the unpleasantness was resolved, Andie added to his troupe. He was joined by such able artists as Jimmy Lynton an excellent "character man" of whom more was said in a previous chapter, and Percy Schoon. There were also Percy Loftus, flute, two brothers Tommy and Teddy Bleasdale who played respectively harp and violin, and Charles Homer who had a fine baritone voice. About this time his fortunes at last changed; it could be said that he became mildly prosperous.

Andie married one of a sister duo act, the other also marrying a Filey man. For many years they lived at 29 Station Road, and had two children, a son and daughter, known affectionately to everyone as Sonny and Girlie. Mrs Caine kept very much in the background as far as the entertainment part of Andie's life was concerned.

In 1913, around Christmas time, Andie opened the first cinema in Filey, in what was previously the Grand Hall in Union Street. On the opening day Father Christmas (Andie of course) handed a gift to every child present. He had always been openhanded with children, and genuinely cared for them. For the excited band of youngsters who invariably skipped and danced around the troupe when they marched from their digs to the sands, and between performances, there were always sweets in his pockets, and sometimes if they were lucky a treat of ice cream.

His morning shows, throughout his career were largely directed towards children. Often there was a weekly talent contest with a prize for the winner on Friday. Andie always encouraged the children to participate with familiar sing-along choruses. This fondness for the younger element was probably attributable to his own childhood spent in an orphanage.

*Andie Caine's Royal Filey Pierrots. Andie is pictured third from left with the dog.*

*Andie Caine's Pierrots, 1914.*

The performances on the sands continued, but as he prospered Andie acquired the Southdenes Pavilion which he enlarged and converted into a theatre. This little theatre was very conveniently situated for the visitors to the Royal Crescent Hotel. As previously remarked, this was much favoured by distinguished visitors including, on occasion, Royalty, and was at one time patronised regularly by the Mountbatten family.

Andie began to give evening shows at the little Southdenes Theatre which were regularly attended by the patrons of the Royal, and in view of this he decided to call his pierrots the Royal Pierrots. The troupe performed in Filey throughout the First World War. Being by this time in his late forties, Andie was not eligible for war service, and his record was unbroken as he continued to provide entertainment throughout the intervening years up to the beginning of the Second World War in 1939.

Amongst those who appeared with his show were Fred Musson who was billed as "The Yorkshire Hebrew Comedian From Leeds". Fred served during the First World War with the armed forces and along with other well known troupers from the ranks of the pierrots was a member of the famous Bing Boys in 1914. He later formed a troupe which played in Leeds at Roundhay Park, a very popular inland pierrot venue. There was Carl Edwards, a vocalist and competent entertainer, and Lister Reekie who was later to become the Editor of the local newspaper *The Filey News*, a publication which is sadly no longer in existence. He held this position for many years and never failed to give the pierrots a write up every season, commenting on the various turns usually in a complimentary manner, but occasionally adding a modicum of constructive criticism, being obviously qualified to comment.

Joe Brook, who proudly laid claim to the title "Yorkshire's Own Bass Baritone", stirred many a lady's heart with his renditions of favourite numbers.

In the early days Andie does not appear to have employed female performers, but eventually a tragic young lady called Lil Marjorie was engaged. Lil was a soubrette but was not very robust and was destined to die at an early age. Later in the thirties there were the Keutie Sisters, Betty and Molly who came from Hull. They were good all-round dancers, a useful addition to any troupe, but were really an acrobatic speciality act. They helped out in the sketches and sang as a trio with an accomplished singer who was currently appearing with the troupe, Wally Cliffe. Other members of the company at this time were Billy Gill, a very fine singer and Tom Hall who acted as "feed' to the resident comic, Gus Yelrob (real name Borley) another Leeds man. Tom also sang comic songs, a classic example being a ditty which rejoiced in the title *Have You Anything On To-night Martha Darling?* which like many of the songs of this period sounds rather naughty but were invariably quite innocent, these being family shows. He was also extremely adept at involving the children in the performance, which no doubt endeared him to Andie.

Johnny Baxter was a real asset to the company, having previously appeared with Catlin's, and Fred Clements' Skegness Pierrots. He was also a well known performer on the music hall circuits.

Johnnie Walsh, the long suffering and ever-patient pianist (who was often called upon to repeat choruses over and over ad nauseam at shows for children)

*Andie Caine's Pierrots prior to Second World War. From left, standing: Billy Gill, Lew Camwell, John Walsh (pianist). From left, seated: Tom Hall, Andie Caine and Gus Yelrob.*

was a well known personality in Filey. He joined Andie in the early thirties, remaining with him until the outbreak of hostilities in 1939. His wife recalls these days with some nostalgia. Pierrots were never well paid, so Johnnie and his wife closed up their home in Leeds during the season and she supplemented the family income by selling ice cream, and by other seasonal jobs, but she remembers these years with affection. In the winter they returned to their home and Johnnie took any engagements that were offered.

It was at this period that the middle-class habit of renting a house for the season reached its zenith. There was in Filey, during the thirties, a particular lady who came unfailingly every season. She loved the pierrots and never missed a performance. During these sessions she sat in a deck chair and industriously knitted whilst enjoying the show. At the end of the season she ultimately presented every member of the troupe with a beautiful hand-knitted sweater.

The troupe employed a local man known as "t'barrier man" to push their piano on a handcart onto the sand every day. The performances were often disrupted when the tide caught up with them causing all "to make a run for it" much to the delight of the children.

Apart from gifts received from such appreciative members of the public as the lady who knitted, on Benefit Nights at the end of the season, Andie divided the whole of the proceeds amongst the members of his company. As one might expect the Benefits were always extremely well patronised.

In Filey, on Lifeboat Day, it became a tradition for the whole company to tour the town collecting for the local lifeboat. Individuals gave miniature impromptu performances in all parts of the town, thus increasing the generosity of the public.

Andie became a man of property; apart from his theatre and cinema he owned two large boarding houses. He served as a Town Councillor and was actively involved in the affairs of the local hospital. He died on the 22nd of November 1941 and was buried in the church-yard of St. Oswald's Church in Filey. A most fitting tribute in the form of a white marble headstone was erected; the inscription reads:

In Sacred Memory
of
Andie Caine
Died 22 Nov 1941
Respected in Life
Lamented in Death

Under this inscription there is a small carving of a conical pierrot hat complete with pom poms.

Andie Caine in his heydey was a real performer, and had the joy of entertaining several decades. The children who originally laughed their way through the early performances, and danced round the pierrots for sweets, were in turn to bring their own children, and often their grandchildren to see the great man. Andie certainly had the record for the most consecutive seasons in any one town on the Yorkshire coast, and undisputedly delighted a record number of holidaymakers. Truly an enviable reputation.

*Andie Caine's grave in Filey churchyard. Note the carving of a Pierrot cap at the base.*

# BRIDLINGTON

Bridlington, in the opinion of many people, has one of the finest sweeps of sand on the Yorkshire coast. The town itself is regarded as one of the earliest watering places in the region.

The medieval market town was not a seaside town, being established about a mile inland towards the Wolds. The only surviving landmark from the fourteenth century settlement is the Bayle which was the Gatehouse of the Augustinian Priory. This was the only part of the foundation to escape the ravages perpetuated at the time of the Dissolution of the Monasteries during the reign of Henry VIII. Most of the houses were on High Street, and the present day dwellings were built over a period spanning almost two centuries from the seventeenth to the nineteenth.

The dignified Old Town, which includes the majestic Priory Church, has over the years become united with the frivolous holiday complex which evolved round the harbour.

There was originally a small settlement round the harbour, consisting of fisherfolk and craftsmen. It was in this vicinity that Robert Fowler, a Quaker, built a ship in 1657. He and eleven followers sailed for America. No one in the company had any knowledge of the skills of navigation, and when they reached their destination they modestly claimed to have steered their ship by prayer.

The harbour divides the town into two bays. North Bay culminates in the rocks of Sewerby and Flamborough, with its lighthouse, and South Bay is dominated by the Spa. Both bays have splended Esplanades, and each over the years has offered a diversity of entertainments.

In the 1880's the Parade was a popular place with visitors and residents alike. There was a bandstand, and over the years many famous orchestras and musicians performed there. It was the place to "see and be seen" on Sunday mornings after church. Everyone wore their finery and it was unheard of to appear on the Parade in any garment mildly resembling recreational or holiday apparel, such as a blazer. Formal dress was without exception the only mode if one wished to remain socially acceptable.

At the south end of the Parade were the Victoria Rooms which housed the Refreshment Rooms; here tea was politely sipped and cakes daintily consumed.

A very popular diversion at this time was the Firework Display. Apart from the usual rockets and showers there were also elaborate and complex set pieces which varied on each occasion.

Electric lighting was installed on the Parade in 1890. As this was the first place in town to possess this amenity a great deal of interest was aroused, and for a season, viewing of this wondrous new mode of illumination was an added attraction.

There were, of course, the usual street entertainments beloved of the Victorians and later Edwardians. There was the Barrel organ usually referred to as a "hurdy gurdy", which churned out the popular songs through the turning of a handle. Itinerant tumblers and fire eaters were in competition with the ever-popular performing animals such as birds, dogs and exotic European bears.

This was the milieu into which the minstrels and later the pierrots made their appearance. The attractions already offered on the beach were the Punch and Judy show, and the donkeys hired out for many years by Mrs Knaggs, to the delight of many a child some of whom came back for rides year after year. The Knaggs family were proprietors of livery stables in Bridlington for many years.

The Spa in the South Bay, as in many other resorts, became over the years a centre for entertainment and housed many delightful seaside shows from 1907 onwards.

The Pavilion which was also built in 1907 was the venue of numerous shows, including pierrot troupes until it burned down in 1935. Like its neighbours on the east coast, Bridlington built a Floral Hall, although not until 1920 after the Armistice, much later than the others. Due to the wide diversity of venues the standard of entertainment was extremely high, as each place vied for the favour of the visitors.

The harbour, apart from supporting the local fishermen, and providing anchorage for a motley assortment of craft, provided fishing trips for visitors, and more important in our context, the pleasure steamers.

There were musicians on the pleasure boats from the early days when *Friends* and the *Frenchman* took parties for a cruise up the coast, and ultimately the *Yorkshireman* which was a familiar treat to many of us more recently.

Wagonettes and horse-drawn charabancs were available to convey the holidaymakers on excursions to Hornsea, Flamborough and Bempton cliffs to see the famous climbers gathering their harvest of sea bird's eggs. These excursions were of course punctuated by eagerly awaited stops for refreshment, often provided in the garden of a private house on route.

In these halcyon days, Princess Parade, named after Princess Mary, a visitor to the town, was beautifully laid out with bright, well-designed flower beds and the much admired floral clock, which was replanted each year to the delight of the public. The Floral Hall was always beautifully decorated; sadly these features in recent years have been sacrificed to make way for a funfare.

As the two original settlements increased in size they each expanded with the building of houses designed to accommodate the growing number of visitors following the advent of the Hull to Bridlington railway in 1846. There are still many of these fine three and four storey terrace houses accommodating visitors today. The railway station was ideally centrally placed.

Like its neighbour Scarborough, Bridlington attracted visitors from the West Riding heavy woollen towns, and has always been a popular resort with the people of Holderness. This meant that there has always been a fairly even balance of townspeople and country folk such as farmers and agricultural workers during the summer season.

The Waterloo Minstrels were possibly the first regular troupe to provide seasonal entertainment in Bridlington. They performed in blackface and wore striped blazers and straw hats. They gave their first shows in the 1890's just

*The Waterloo Pierrots Original Troupe.*

*The Waterloo Pierrots on their pitch in 1905. Note the harp.*

before the turn of the century. The Waterloo's took their name from the Waterloo Restaurant in Garrison Street, where the owner Jack Grantham allowed them to store their costumes on the premises and dress for their shows. He is said to have been pleased and flattered by the adoption of the name of his establishment. They may have helped to promote business as he was apparently renowned for his offer of a "good cuppa for tuppence".

The usual pitch of the Waterloo Minstrels was on the beach in front of the old wooden sea defences. When the tide was in, making beach performances impossible, they toured the streets giving a mobile show in front of the hotels and often collecting from them.

In due course the blazers were abandoned for the now popular pierrot pom poms and ruffles and with the traditional white faces they became the Waterloo Pierrots. In 1909 they took over the pitch on Beaconsfield and gave their shows in a tin-roofed wooden building.

Charlie Beanland (The Guvnor) was known to one and all as "Sammy", and to the children as Uncle Sam. The first troupe was made up of his brother Joe or Johanna, H.B. Coda, Charles Danton, and Fred Carey. Their musical accompaniment was a harp and fiddle which those who have memories of those days have declared to be particularly shrill and penetrating.

The Beanland brothers were born in Morecambe. Charles Henry Beanland was an accomplished comedian, his first appearance on Bridlington beach being with Catlin's troupe in the early 1890's as a comic. Andie Caine who was to become famous for his Filey pierrots was also with this troupe.

The stage careers of both brothers began when they toured the Halls as a comedy duo billed as Beanland and Bath Lightning Cartoonists, Joe being the Bath half of the team. Joseph Dearlove Beanland, or Johanna, appears mainly on the theatre bills as Bath, and also on some of the pierrot programmes. He was well known for his lightning caricatures and expert handling of tissue paper from which he produced in seconds elaborate lacy tablecloths and dresses.

It was during one of these tours with his brother that Joe met his future wife. She was part of an act who called themselves the "Sisters Geraldine", dancers and comediennes, by the name of Florrie and May. Joe and Florrie were married at St. John's Church in Manchester on the 30th of April 1902. May also married a performer, Laurie Mellin, otherwise Kyoto, who had a conjuring act and was also well known as a pantomime cat. Joe and his wife set up home in Bridlington at 15 Hazelmere Avenue, and had two sons.

Charlie was less fortunate in his domestic arrangements. He made an unhappy marriage and eventually divorced his first wife who treated him badly. He was later to find happiness with a comedienne called Marlie Caird, who was much younger than him, and they worked together in some of Charlie's later productions including "Frills and Flounces" which he ran in London in 1921.

The Waterloo's began to amuse the holidaymakers in 1893 and at that time there was little or no opposition. The Spa and Pavilion had not been built; although a drama was occasionally presented at the Victoria Rooms it posed no real threat to them.

H.B. Coda who stayed with the Beanlands in some capacity for about twenty years played the violin, and acted in the sketches. When Charlie went into

*Charles Beanland (Uncle Sammy)*
*of the Waterloo Pierrots.*

*Marlie Caird, wife of Charles Beanland,*
*of the Waterloo Pierrots.*

*Charles Beanland's Frills and Flounces, 1921.*

*The Waterloo Pierrots, 1912.*

theatre management in later years, Coda directed the music for the shows. Charlie was at one period in the 1930's in partnership with another veteran pierrot, Harry Russell. They produced pantomimes in Huddersfield and various other venues.

Charlie Danton was another ex-Catlin man. He sometimes used the name Carson, and spent several seasons with the Waterloo's at Bridlington. Like Chas Beanland, he eventually went into theatre management at the Rotherham Hippodrome. Other regulars were Fred Carey, or Longfellow, as he was known, and George Hyams who joined them in the early days and stayed with the show.

At various times other artists joined the boys, but this little group stayed together for many seasons. The visitors knew them all by name and regarded them as personal friends, often coming back year after year to renew their acquaintance and stroll along the sea front with them between performances. One noteworthy addition for the occasional season was Jack Hylton. His father was a cotton spinner, who subsidised his meagre income by singing comic songs at Smoking Concerts; later he became the landlord of a public house. At the age of ten young Jack was appearing as "The Singing Mill Boy" complete with clogs , and in 1905 he became a boy vocalist with the pierrots during the summer season, and sang in his father's pub in winter. He later performed as a pianist and became a musician of note in the 1930's. After the Second World War he presented his own seaside shows.

Like all beach performers the Waterloo's had their problems with the tide. On one occasion, which was recorded for posterity by an enterprising photographer who happened to be present, they mistimed their show and the sea encroached, washing away their stage. The boys dashed into the sea in full costume to retrieve it and as they walked out in an extremely bedraggled state the fortunate camera man recorded the scene. The photograph later appeared in the *Police Gazette* with an amusing caption.

68

The troupe stayed together until the outbreak of war in 1914, when sadly they went their different ways. Charlie, as already stated, with his wife Marlie went to London and for the rest of his life concentrated on theatre production and management. He spent the last years of his life in Morecambe with his sisters Cissie and Polly. After Marlie died he often spent the winter months with Joe and his wife in Bridlington. Ultimately Charlie was diagnosed as having cancer, and was devotedly nursed by his sisters and Cissie's husband, Albert Fells, ending his days in Morecambe where he was born.

Joe who was a Freemason and by now a well-respected member of Bridlington society became the manager of the Roxy cinema on Quay Road when the troupe split up. He stayed for many years but was eventually forced to retire when his sight failed, dying in Bridlington in February 1931.

Will and Tom Catlin both appeared in Bridlington in the early days. Will developed a certain attachment to the resort. In the early years of the century between Easter and Whitsuntide, Catlin's Royal Pierrots always did four or five weeks on the sands where they were just as popular as they were at Scarborough.

Contemporary with the Waterloo Pierrots were the Beaconsfield Singers, a five man group, each in his own way talented. The one who is still remembered today, however, is Will Turner. Will had been born with a deformed leg, but in no way did this deter him from his chosen profession as an entertainer. He pluckily capitalised on this defect, and this was never more appropriate than when he clumped around the stage during his rendition of *At Trinity Church I Met My Doom*, adding to the "drama" of the piece. Will was the original performer of this Music Hall favourite which was written by Fred Gilbert in 1894.

The song was taken up by Birmingham born comedian and vocalist Tom Costello. During his long and successful variety career he sang innumerable songs, but was best remembered for his performance of this one. He also performed the song with the same uneven gait as Will Turner.

The Beaconsfield Singers took their name from the site on which they performed which in later years became a bowling green. There was a stage with a wooden fence round it known as the Summer Gardens. In 1909 they vacated this pitch and it was taken over by the Waterloo's who performed on the sands during the day and on the stage in the evenings.

Charles Palmer came to Bridlington at the beginning of the century with his wife Peggy Walsh who was a dancer. The Corporation employed him as manager of the Royal Princess Parade including the Victoria Rooms and the Floral Pavilion. He modernised the stage at the Victoria Rooms, adding special lighting and other facilities not normally provided in provincial theatres, in an attempt to encourage London companies to perform in the town. Many prestigious actors and actresses came to Bridlington at this period, but the plays in no way rivalled the pierrots.

At the Floral Pavilion Charley offered entertainment of a completely different type. It was here that he engaged concert parties including pierrots. The shows ranged from Tom Carrick's "White Musketeers" who were extremely popular, largely due to Tom himself who rendered his parodies of popular

*The Smart Set Entertainers. Walter George is pictured far right.*

songs with great effect and won many a supporter with his Yorkshire humour usually delivered with a comic pathos that was specifically his own.

Equally popular was Walter George's "Smart Set". This was a group of five men and four ladies. They were a costume concert party and dressed "for the act", but their standard dress was blazers and straw boaters for the men, and pretty Edwardian dresses and hats for the ladies. One of the star performers was Miss Georgie Martin. A song which was regularly featured in their repertoire was the *Teddy Bear Song.*

> He's my darling Teddy Bear,
> Just a big, big Teddy Bear
> Soft and pearly, brown and curly,
> He's my darling Teddy Bear.

Other favourites at this period were Harry Montague's "Vagabonds" and Charles Heslop's "Brownies".

Flockton Foster achieved popularity with his shows on the west coast. The visitors to Blackpool and St. Annes were familiar with his costume concert parties. In 1906 when the Grand Pavilion opened, his "Idols" were among the concert parties engaged by Charles Palmer.

Flockton Foster excelled in the delivery of monologues and he introduced the Yorkshire audiences to such gems as *Gunga Din* and *The Green Eye of the Little Yellow God,* which were later to be popularised on radio by that great reciter, Bransby Williams. Foster had a ready wit and was quick to parody the songs of the period with his own amusing renditions using such unusual ploys as Dog Latin which, perhaps surprisingly, were enthusiastically received. His association with Bridlington was to last for many years. By the late 1920's and

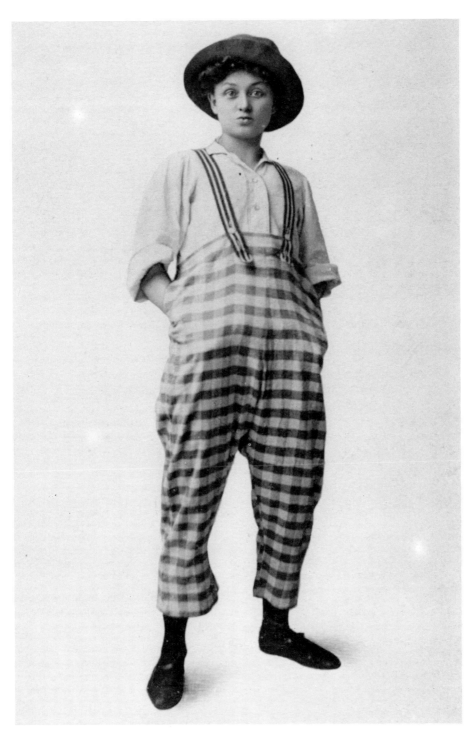

*Miss Georgie Martin of the Smart Set Entertainers.*

# H. FLOCKTON-FOSTER,
### PRODUCER MANAGER.

*Just concluded his 6th Season as Producer-Manager of the SUPER SUMMER RESIDENT COMPANY at Bridlington, with usual success.*

*YOU may, sometime, require a Manager-Producer who has a comprehensive experience, and the highest credentials, who KNOWS his business—and DOES it—and who can write and revise script and melodies.*

#### RECENT RESIDENT PANTOMIMES
*Written and Produced, include :-*
*Cardiff - Newport—Huddersfield—Reading.*

*Other Productions (1934) include :-*
*" Princess Charming "          " Our Miss Gibbs "*
*" The Creaking Chair "*

#### 53 MILLBROOK ROAD———BRIXTON,
#### LONDON, S.W. 9.

*An example of an entertainer's card which was sent to various booking agents.*

early 1930's he had become the producer manager of his own Summer Shows in the resort, and was writing and producing his own pantomimes in various towns.

With the advent of radio and its growing popularity as receiver sets became increasingly available to most households, a new type of entertainment entered the lives of the public. Fred Rayne called his concert party the "North Regionals", presumably because they frequently did broadcasts from the old North Regional Station of the B.B.C. In the early days programmes were regionally focused rather than the nationally networked four channels to which we are accustomed today.

Fred Rayne and his troupe appeared in various resorts on the north east coast including Redcar in the 1930's, but it would seem that they favoured Bridlington where they performed at the Floral Pavilion for several seasons. The holidaymakers were delighted to be able to see "in the flesh" the performers to whom they listened to on the wireless. The novelty of putting a face to a voice, and bragging to their friends that they had seen this or that person was something very few could resist.

One of the members of Fred Rayne's troupe who entertained holidaymakers in the carefree pre-war days was a young lady who was destined to become a star of stage, film, radio and television. Her name was Beryl Reid now familiar to most of us for her radio character Marlene, and later for her sterling performances in such films as *Entertaining Mr Sloane* and *The Killing of Sister George*.

In the late 1930's Fred Rayne changed the name of his show from the "North Regionals" to the "Parade Show", no doubt in honour of the famous Parade at Bridlington. The original concert party consisted of four ladies and six men. They wore a variety of costumes including the traditional pom poms and ruffles. The "Parade Show" had nine members, four men and five ladies.

*Fred Rayne's North Regionals. Fred Rayne is seated centre.*

*Harry Benet's Gaiety Fayre Company, 1946, the forerunner of today's sophisticated seaside shows.*

73

Several of the performers were the same but by the this time Beryl Reid appears to have moved on, no doubt to take another step towards her glittering future.

In the aftermath of war the holidaymakers in Bridlington, as in other resorts, were looking for a more sophisticated type of show. It was in this atmosphere in 1946 that Harry Benet presented his "Gaiety Fayre" company at the Grand Pavilion.

This was a lavish production with elaborate sets and glamorous costumes, deliberately tailored to appeal to the audiences who had recently lived through the austerity and deprivations of six years of war with all its restrictions and uncertainty. People now desired to rid themselves of the constraints of "Utility" clothing and domestic furnishings.

Basically there were ten members of the company: Charles Douglas, Pat McKay, Freddie Foss, Reg Kinsman, Rupert Keppel and Bertie Rich. The ladies were Lillian McEvoy, Mary Lynton, Stella Halles and Trixie Tatton. There were also four young ladies who called themselves the "Society Four", and the "Flora Dora Girls" who provided the chorus line.

This was so patently far removed from the simple and joyous spontaneous entertainment provided by the pierrots and was surely the forerunner of the star-studded extravaganza of today, no longer truly seaside entertainment.

# HORNSEA

Hornsea is mentioned in the Domesday Book, the name then being Hornessi, which was Old Norse in origin and points to the fact that the invaders were probably the original settlers. Hornsea was originally a fishing village and the dwellings were concentrated round the lake or Mere. The Mere is said to be the largest fresh water lake in Yorkshire, and now provides the angler and naturalist with an ideal environment, although in the days of the Abbots it was, of course, a poacher's paradise.

With the growing interest in seaside holidays the village expanded in the direction of the sea, and became an attractive resort with a pleasant esplanade, and a fine sandy beach. With the advent of the visitors, however, the fishing industry declined.

One of the first signs of change occurred in the 1820's when a few bathing machines appeared on the beach; there was also a chalybeate spring which encouraged hopes of a spa, which for some unfortunate reason failed to materialise. By the mid 1850's Hornsea had become a popular resort with the people of Hull, being at that period a quiet and peaceful little place.

In 1864, after innumerable setbacks, the Hull and Hornsea Railway ran its first train from Wilmington Station in Hull. This was a real gala day. There was a local band in the first carriage of the train, and people lined the route to cheer the train on its way. It arrived at Hornsea one hour after its departure from Wilmington, a vast improvement on the three hours taken by the horse and cart which had hitherto been the usual mode of transport. The railway altered the whole character of the place, as the trains ran an hourly service in either direction. A day out for the tripper was now an attractive proposition and in the holiday season special fares were offered as an added inducement.

No doubt influenced by neighbouring resorts who were building piers, the Town Council in their infinite wisdom decided that such a structure would add to the attractions of Hornsea as a resort. Joseph Armytage Wade was the man who gave the town its pier. In 1897 the ill-fated construction was completed. It was built by the Hornsea Pier Company and claimed to be the first one in the county to be completed. The now familiar story of the storm of 1880 with its attendant trail of destruction was to prove the downfall of the project. The ship *The Earl of Derby* collided with the pier having been blown off course by the phenomenal winds. The pavilion at the seaward end was completely demolished, and several feet of the ironwork girders were washed away. What remained of this once pleasant amenity now became more of an eyesore than an attraction. The final ignominy occurred in 1910 when demolition was finally completed.

In 1905, when schemes for reconstruction of the pier were abandoned, the money which had been set aside for this was used instead for improving the Promenade and building of the Floral Hall, which is still in use today.

75

## "HULL TIMES" WEEKLY CARTOON.

### ON THE SANDS, HORNSEA.
THE ABOVE WAS SKETCHED AT HORNSEA RECENTLY, BY ONE OF OUR SPECIAL ARTISTS.

*A topical cartoon of the period.*

The railway, now well established, not only transported the trippers on their excursion trains, but having provided a regular and frequent service encouraged people from Hull to move house and live by the sea commuting daily to work. This was really the foundation of the pleasant country town which we know today. It was in this environment that the pierrots achieved their popularity, both with visitors and residents around the turn of the century, and continued to delight their adherents for several decades.

In the summer of 1903 the Royal Bohemians Concert Party entertained the holidaymakers in Hornsea. These six gentlemen were elegantly clad in stockings and satin knee breeches which were tied with bows. They had matching jackets which were left open and under these they wore white shirts with ruffles at the neck and wrist, arranged over the neck of the jacket and outside the sleeves. On their feet they wore buckled shoes. They favoured the traditional skull cap as headgear. Like most of the troupes of that period they used a piano for accompaniment.

In 1904 The Lawn in Hornsea was the venue during the summer season for Spot's Jolly Japs, five men who sported bright floral kiminos and oriental hats. The kimino seems to have had a fairly wide appeal as a costume for seaside

*Early entertainers on the lawn at Hornsea, Spot's Jolly Japs.*

troupes of this period, as quite a few groups favoured it in other parts of the country, a classic example being George Hall's Merry Imps who appeared at Morecambe. One of their members was Billy Bass who became the well known comedian Billy Danvers.

Of all the entertainers who appeared on the beach and promenade over the years at Hornsea, the most noteworthy was, without doubt, Harry Russell. His career in the entertainment business spanned some sixty years, during which time he won the admiration and respect not only of his audiences, but of his fellow artistes.

His shows, whether the summer pierrot performances at the seaside, or in later years lavish pantomime productions, were always well constructed and presented in an extremely professional manner.

Harry Russell was born in Grimsby in 1877. His surname was Barry, a little known fact, as most people were more familiar with his stage name of Russell. His father was a Doctor of Music who had obtained his degree from Trinity College, Dublin. He was a well known figure in musical circles, and was also a classical scholar in Greek, Latin and Hebrew. This was the background in which young Harry spent his formative years, and was doubtless a contributory factor to his success as a scriptwriter and producer when he formed his own concert party and in later years wrote and produced his own pantomime in his own theatre.

By 1895, then in his late teens, he was already gaining valuable experience with various small companies throughout the country, appearing as a comedian with some measure of success.

In 1897 he appeared in his home town of Grimsby with a company called the Victoria Minstrels. There were seven members in this troupe: Mr. Interlocuter

77

*Harry Russell.*

*Harry Russell and his Company in the sketch "The Home Made Car". Harry Russell is pictured second from right.*

was A.B. Stills, Tambos were A. Skelton, B. Moon, and H. Coultas, Bones were H. Russell, J. Harris and G. Croft.

Arthur Skelton was a female impersonator of some note and his impressions of Marie Lloyd and Marie Loftus were much requested. Harry Russell as a comedian had by now developed a robust style and a ready wit, which was greatly relished by north country audiences. There is no record of his family's reaction to his appearance in Grimsby. In 1901 his talents received recognition when he won the first prize in the Professional Variety Artists Competition at the Middlesex Theatre of Varieties in Drury Lane. He wrote a comedy sketch entitled "T'Man Fra' Pudsey". Oswald Stoll presented the sketch and Harry played John Willie Weeks, the man from Pudsey. He loved this character and included him in many of his shows.

Harry Russell now had no difficulty in finding professional engagements and appeared in the Halls with such luminaries as Kate Collins, G.H. Elliott, George Robey and Dan Leno. It was at this period that Harry wrote his first summer show which he produced on the Hoe at Plymouth for two or three seasons. He called his troupe Harry Russell's Popular Pierrots, which consisted of T.H. Biddick, musician; Beatrice Royle, singer comedienne; W. Pettitt, banjo; E. Harcourt, singer; and the Sisters Sylvia, soubrettes. Harry provided the laughs including his beloved "John Willie Weeks".

In 1907 Harry came north again and produced a summer show at Hornsea, called Harry Russell's Cadets and Concert Party. They performed at the north end of the promenade. The troupe was composed of six men and a charming lady called Verna Reed. The men wore white trousers and smart double-breasted blazers, black bow ties and yachting caps. This was a style of dress almost as much favoured as the pom poms and ruffles by some seaside performers. With Harry in this show were two friends from the earlier days of the concert parties, Neville Delmar and Bert Gordon. The shows were written and produced by Harry, sometimes in collaboration with his friends, and included a sketch called "'The Home Made Motor Car" which was a great favourite with both residents and holidaymakers alike, and like "John Willie" appeared with regularity in the programme. The troupe appeared at Hornsea for several seasons and Harry was often heard to say in later years that the time he spent in the resort with his summer shows was the happiest time in his life.

Harry went back to the Halls for a period and it was at this time that he started to write scripts for pantomime. His last appearance with a seaside show was in his thirties when he appeared with Andie Caine at Filey in 1914. Harry married an ex-Tiller Girl whose stage name was Madge Allen. They were an extremely successful team. He wrote the scripts for his excellent pantomime productions and appeared as principal comedian with Madge as his Principal Boy. They had a son Allan, who was to follow in his father's footsteps as a producer.

In 1922 he opened his theatre the "New Arcadia" in Doncaster, and was always willing to support local charities giving assistance where needed and rapidly becoming a much respected citizen of the town. Catlin's Pierrots were regular performers at his theatre, and no doubt remembering his own days as a

*The Reps Concert Party, 1923.*

seaside performer he welcomed touring seaside shows during the winter months, before and after his pantomimes.

Despite the fact that he had been in poor health for some time, his condition gradually deteriorating, he appeared with his own road show in the summer of 1941. Preparations were well advanced for pantomimes in Halifax and Norwich, but during the latter half of September he suffered a stroke which was to prove fatal. On the evening of Saturday the 27th of September 1941 at the time when he would have been "taking the Curtain" at the close of the week's performance, he slipped peacefully away at his home in Bessacar. He was mourned by many, including a number of performers to whom he had extended a helping hand in the furtherance of their careers.

In the period before the First World War, Harry East's Novelties appeared as an open-air show, but in the post war period they came back and gave their shows in the Floral Hall.

In the summer of 1923 the Reps concert party set up their stage on the beach. The troupe consisted of four men, one of whom was a drummer, and two ladies. The men wore the traditionally shaped pierrot suits, the difference being that they were made from brightly coloured printed material with plain sleeves. They sported white ruffles about their necks and wore skull caps. The ladies' dresses were of the same print, stylishly cut in the fashion of the period and topped with saucy little hats of the same material.

During the years leading up to the outbreak of the Second World War, numerous concert parties appeared at Hornsea with varying success, but there were none who returned consistently season after season in the true pierrot tradition, reminiscent of the days of Harry Russell.

# WITHERNSEA

The present town of Withernsea was originally two villages, Owthorpe and Withernsea. In the early years of the nineteenth century the coast erosion, which is a constant threat to the north eastern coast today, had eaten away large areas of land and consequently the population of each village had been drastically reduced to a few souls in each area. In 1816 Owthorpe Church, which had been precariously balanced at the edge of the cliff since the end of the eighteenth century, finally crashed down onto the beach. The church at Withernsea had already been claimed by the sea in the fifteenth century, and another church had been built, but the population was so sparse that it was impossible to find funds to keep it in good repair.

These two communities were finally united under the administration of one town council in the 1890's. It was at this period that Withernsea also began to develop into a very popular holiday resort.

When Victoria became Queen in the mid-nineteenth century, there was also a perceptible increase in the population of the villages, which were at the constant mercy of the sea. The threat from erosion was more serious on this part of the coast than in other areas, as the sea had already pushed its way inland to the meres or lakes which existed in both villages, swallowing up a considerable portion of land in the process. The terrain was flat and there were no protective cliffs to halt its advance. The beach now sloped straight down. The enormity of this advance can be estimated by the peat deposits which were originally at the bottom of the meres, and occasionally emerge at very low tide off the North Promenade.

In 1851 Anthony Bannister, who was the Mayor of the town, envisaged the possibilities of a railway, and the Hull and Holderness Railway Company was formed. Its officials had high hopes for Withernsea. Not only would the railway be invaluable to the farmers of Holderness, but the directors were far-sighted in their perception of the lucrative tourist trade, which was to gain momentum around the turn of the century.

Withernsea had all the advantages necessary for an ideal terminus; the lack of cliffs was a unique attraction, giving easy access to the beach as the visitors alighted at the station. A sea wall was built in an attempt to halt the erosion, and it was decided that the town should have a pier. This was obviously designed to attract the holidaymakers, with its quarter mile of promenade and a saloon, but there were also plans to use it for landing fish for sending direct to Hull by rail.

Unfortunately this amenity was short lived; being built in the years 1875-78, it suffered the same ignominious fate as the other piers of the north east coast during the great storm of 1880. By 1900 only fifty feet of the pier and the imposing castellated ornamental gate remained. In 1910, after various mishaps, the rest of the pier was removed leaving only the gate which was already a favourite pitch with the pierrots, as obviously it was not at the mercy of the tides which often interrupted their shows on the beach, where for some years now they had been delighting visitors and residents alike.

The enormous Queen's Hotel which had been built at the rear of the railway station to accommodate the expected influx of visitors proved unsuccessful. It was too large, and too costly. The many boarding houses, which were more homely and suited the pockets of the majority of visitors, were more popular.

Fortunately in 1892, the Queen's Hotel was bought by Francis and Sir James Reckitt, and presented to Hull Royal Infirmary to be used as a convalescent home for the poor families of Hull. Sir James later provided a sanatorium for tuberculosis sufferers in the grounds, as the air of Withernsea was deemed to be extremely bracing and beneficial. Not only did this enterprise bring the patients to the town, but also their families and friends who visited regularly, thus increasing trade. The hospital was at one period very ably administered by Matron Cavell whose sister Edith was martyred by the Germans when she was executed during the First World War.

Apart from the joys of "sea, sands and sunshine" which featured in its advertising slogan, Withernsea had much to offer in its early years as a resort. There were pleasant promenades both north and south of the Pier, and numerous areas had been converted into pleasant lawns and well-stocked colourful flower beds to delight the eye. Each promenade had its band performances to please the ear, and close to the station were the Pleasure Gardens where one could sit under the trees and listen to the music whilst enjoying various forms of refreshment; and there was, of course the Floral Hall, which over the years provided a very wide range of seaside entertainment, including the pierrot shows.

The close proximity of the beach to the Railway Station made it an ideal spot to spread out a picnic. There were the usual stalls in the area round the Pier, jugs of tea being in constant demand, with ice cream being almost as popular. There was a play area with swings and other delights for the children, including of course the patient donkeys at the beach end of Seaside Road.

The pierrots were very much in evidence; apart from the pier gate there was a pitch on the beach near the steps leading from the North Promenade Bandstand. The audiences for these shows were often swelled on the warm summer evenings by people who came in on the evening excursion trains from Hull.

One of the earliest pierrot troupes to appear at Withernsea was, not surprisingly, Will Catlin. Will, having realised the advantages of presenting shows in more than one resort concurrently, found Withernsea ideal. As has been previously mentioned around the turn of the century he had explored the resorts along the Yorkshire coast with varying success, but Withernsea proved to be a real triumph. The railway had ensured that the town was always well patronised by holiday makers and the Council was showing an interest in improving the amenities offered to attract visitors. As usual Will's assessment of the situation was sound, and Catlin's Pierrots were to be part of the Withernsea scene for many a season.

Obviously Will could not direct every troupe personally, and he appointed

# CATLIN'S ROYAL PIERROTS

## GIVE ENTERTAINMENTS DAILY
### During the Summer Season, at the following places:—

## Arcadia, Scarboro.
MANAGER, MR. W. CATLIN.

## Arcadia, Colwyn Bay.
MANAGER, MR. SID FRERE.

## Beach Pavilion, Bournemouth
MANAGER, MR. G. HOUGHTON.

## Beach Pavilion, Bournemouth
MANAGER, MR. H. LOVELL.

## Assembly Rooms, Withernsea.
MANAGER, MR. C. MILNER.

## Park Pavilion, Erith.
MANAGER, MR. F. BLYTHE.

## Wellington Pier, Yarmouth.
MANAGER, MR. T. BRAHAM FOX.

*List of Catlin's Managers. Note Charlie Milner for Withernsea.*

managers for his resorts, choosing to remain in Scarborough himself. His choice for Withernsea was Charles Milner. Charles had quite a wide experience of the Halls and had been a member of the Scarborough troupe. He was experienced in management and administration, and was also an extremely versatile performer. His main act was as a character comedian, but he was also a competent dancer, pianist and singer. He was well versed in the type of entertainment that Will Catlin aimed to provide. Born in 1879 young Charles Milner was later apprenticed to a French polisher from whom he learned his trade.

Milner was obsessed with the stage and at the first opportunity he abandoned his trade and devoted himself to a career in entertainment. In 1899 at the age of twenty his hard work was rewarded when he topped the Bill at the Palace of Varieties in Leeds.

When Queen Victoria died in 1901, Charles was appearing at the Alhambra in Porter Street, Hull. The announcement of her demise was made from the stage and the theatre emptied quietly. Charles worked most of the theatres in and around Hull including the Tivoli and the Alexander. When he was appearing at the Empire in Grimston Street, Hull, there was an act who billed himself as "The Man They Couldn't Hang". His name was John Clempart, a Russian born strong man. His act was acknowledged as one of the most daring to be staged at that period. Its success depended upon split second timing. When the assistant pulled the lever which operated the trapdoor on the scaffold, Clempart at lightning speed caught the knot at the back of his head and took the strain before assuming a hanging position. On this particular evening he missed the knot and in full view of the audience really did hang himself. As soon as it was realised what had happened he was cut down and rushed to Hull Royal Infirmary, where his life hung in the balance for some weeks. It was his iron constitution which eventually aided his recovery. As a result of this contretemps, legislation was introduced banning acts of this nature.

It was thought that Charles also had the misfortune to be at the Wood Green Empire in London on the 23rd March, 1918, when, during his performance of his famous bullet catching trick, Chung Ling Soo was fatally wounded on the stage. In happier circumstances Charles appeared on the same bill with such prestigious artists as Vesta Tilley and Dan Leno.

Charles married Jane (Jenny) Arnett whose brother Chas was also a Catlin man, though not appearing with the Withernsea troupe at the time. The family always stayed at the Pier Hotel on Seaside Road during the season, which began at the end of March and extended to September. The Pier Hotel was a pleasant middle class establishment presided over by Mr and Mrs Jack Ramstar.

The Milner family came to the hotel for fourteen seasons and met many interesting people, one of whom was Iron Hague the heavyweight boxer who was training at Withernsea for his forthcoming fight at the National Sporting Club in London with the black American Sam Langford. The fight took place in 1909, Langford proving the victor.

The boys of the troupe stayed with the same landlady every season. She owned a boarding house in Queen Street, and over the years a real family atmosphere evolved. Local friendships were cemented and the arrival of the

*Catlin's Pierrots performing on boards on Withernsea sands, 1910.*

*Catlin's braving the tide, 1910.*

*Catlin's Pierrots at the entrance to the Pier Head Withernsea, 1905.*

pierrots was eagerly awaited every year. They were joined about 1909 by a young local boy called Ernie Preston.

In the early days the pierrots put down the stage on the beach near the North Promenade, but eventually they moved to a pitch in front of the impressive turreted gate which was all that remained of the pier. Like all the pierrot troupes they gave three shows a day, morning, afternoon and evening.

In 1904, during Charles's managership of the Catlin Troupe, the Russian Outrage, or Dogger Bank Incident took place. On Trafalgar Day the 21st of October, the Russian Naval Fleet fired on a fleet of Hull Trawlers fishing at the Dogger Bank in the misconception that they were ships of the Japanese, with whom they were at war.

Six trawlers were hit and several men were injured. The captain of the *Crane*, George Smith, a married man with eight children, and William Legett, third hand, a bachelor, were killed, This incident was condemned as a universal scandal, and needless to say the City of Hull was up in arms.

In the summer season following this event, Catlin's Pierrots, being ever topical, performed a number called *The Russian Bear*. Our illustration shows that they had an easel set up on the pier steps, bearing a dramatic picture of the sinking of the *Crane* whilst the vocalist rendered the song.

In 1909 when King Edward VII died the pierrots performed before a very small audience for the evening show. An enterprising Hull photographer Robert Watson of Anlaby Road had made a film of the funeral. This was rushed through and shown at the Assembly Rooms in Withernsea the same evening, drawing the crowds away from the other attractions.

During the winter seasons Charles Milner entertained with troupes organised

*Ellison's Entertainers, 1912. Pictured far right is Charles Milner, and third from left, Joe Ellison.*

by Will Catlin in Margate and Buxton, taking his wife and family with him. In 1912 Charles appeared in Withernsea with Joe Ellison's Entertainers; Joe also had a troupe in Cleethorpes.

When war broke out in 1914, Charles joined the Iniskilling Fusiliers, serving as an entertainer and also carrying out military duties for the duration. After his return to civilian life, it was no longer easy to find work in the entertainment business, so undaunted he resumed his trade as a French polisher working for Bladon's of Hull; he also handled insurance business for the Prudential part-time. Charles Milner died at his home on Beverley High Road, Hull, aged 72, leaving happy memories of his pierrot days in Withernsea to countless holiday-makers and residents of the town.

The famous Hull comedian, Dick Henderson made one of his first professional appearances with the pierrots on Withernsea beach. Born in Strawberry Street, Dick served his apprenticeship as a fitter at Earle's Shipyard. He had often "done a turn" in the local clubs, but it was his first time with the pierrots that convinced him that he had a future as an entertainer. His judge-ment was, of course, entirely sound. "The Yorkshire Comedian" successfully toured the U.S.A. in Vaudeville during the early 1920's. He appeared in Warner Brothers films and captivated English audiences on his return to his native land. He had the honour of appearing in two Royal Variety Shows and the family tradition was carried on by his son, the late Dickie Henderson.

Another Hull comedian who made his debut on Withernsea beach was Bunny Doyle. In 1908 Bunny was taken to the resort on holiday and entered a talent contest organised by Tadman's Uniques concert party. There was also a

*Tadmans Uniques. Second from left is Doris White of Hull, the dancer.*

young Hull dancer and soubrette named Doris White appearing with the company that season. Bernard (Bunny) Doyle was awarded a prize and he so enjoyed the experience that he set his heart on becoming pierrot; he was to make his first professional appearance at the Bijou Music Hall in Hull and toured the Northern Halls. During the First World War, Bunny served in the West Yorkshire Regiment and was a member of the Duds Concert Party along with Bud Flanagan.

Other early visitors to the town were the Merry Mascots who erected an alfresco on the Beach Lawn and were always sure of a good audience.

In the summers of 1922 and 1923 Horace West's Night Lights appeared at the Unity Hall. The company included a handsome young baritone called Reg Lawrence who regularly brought audiences to their feet with his rendition of *Nirvana*. It is said that he disturbed the hearts of many of the ladies in the town, and had a regular following. He also sang duets with a young lady called Jean Anderson who played the cello. In 1929 Horace West returned to the town, but this time not as leader of the company. Sure of a warm welcome by the many who remembered his previous visits, he appeared at the Floral Hall with Frank A. Terry's Super Optimists.

In 1925 Frank A. Terry, who was an ex Catlin man having appeared at Scarborough in the 1913 show as a baritone, joined forces with Ossie Battye, well known and loved on the West Coast as the "funny man" in Don Hardie's Players who appeared regularly at Morecambe. Frank's wife, Jessie Crone, had been a comedienne with Walter Darling's Fantastics at the Pier Pavilion, Cleethorpes and was a definite asset to the company. Frank employed many stars in the years between the wars, one of whom was to become a well known

*Doris M. White.*

*The Merry Mascots, Beach Lawn.*

entertainer of stage, screen and radio. Harry Korris began his career as a pierrot in 1906 at the age of eighteen at the Onchan Head Pavilion, Isle of Man. He appeared with Will Ambro's Debonairs and Ernest Binn's Merrie Arcadians in his early years. His wife Connie Emerson was a member of Grapho's Jovial Jollies when they met. The show was billed as a remarkable entertainment with eight star artists and three changes of programme, Monday, Wednesday and Friday.

In the early twenties, after the War, there was a revival of interest in pierrots and concert parties. Social historians attribute this to the fact that many entertainers who were now ex-servicemen were unemployed and mostly without hope of work. They banded together and formed concert parties of their own, entertaining the public in every type of venue from the London stage to the small halls and seaside shows.

Perhaps the most celebrated of these concert parties was the Splinters. They were entirely an ex-service group and in France had been billed as "Les Rouges et Noirs".

It was at this period that the First Army Follies came to Withernsea. Some of the artists had been members of the Splinters group. They advertised their show as "Chips" a Revue without a chorus. They claimed "Every artiste a soldier, every soldier an artiste and every Lady a Gentleman". They were of course similar to the female impersonators who grace the shows of today. Since their programme was intended as family entertainment the material was inoffensive, and the public appeared to find them something of a novelty.

The show at the Floral Hall in 1929 (this was not their first production in the town) had a cast of seven versatile entertainers. Roy Byng had appeared with the Splinters as "Annette the Leading Lady", Vivian Taylor was with the very first Splinters troupe and was billed as a "Lady of Many Parts". Lennox Dalton was a brilliant baritone, Dave Gibson was a dancer and Freddie Finch a vocalist who was equally capable of producing a male and female range according to the character he was portraying. Harry Watson did a Scottish act and Will Burns who was a versatile comedian obliged with a choice offering in the form of a portrayal of the wartime cartoon character "Old Bill".

Another group with a similar concept who were equally popular in the town called themselves Pierrots-in-Plus-Fours. They billed themselves as "A War legacy. The Super all male Concert Party in which the weaker sex are portrayed by the stronger".

Henri Harper was a vocalist with a wide range, which aided his dual personality act. Teddie Marty who had been a member of Chips was billed as "The Original Perfect Lady", Gene Oakley was the "Personality Girl" and Max Maxwell provided light comedy. Hastings Conler sang baritone and Geoffrey Hazel and Walter Cross were the company's pianists. They advertised themselves in a similar manner to Chips, "Every artist a Man, Every Man an Artist".

A traditional troupe who appeared in Pierrot Costume at the Floral Hall in 1923 were the Bits 'O Brightness; they were seven in number, four men and three girls.

In the post-war period of the early twenties, as the seaside tradition of entertainment struggled to present an air of normality (in spite of the fact that so many popular and talented entertainers had fallen or had been disabled during the war) Withernsea attracted many concert parties. Some of the entertainers remembered its friendly atmosphere from happier days, others new to the town, came to try their luck and stayed for numerous seasons or returned on more than one occasion in the ensuing years between the two wars.

A group which maintained its popularity in this manner was Doug Cranston's Epics. They gave nightly shows at the Floral Hall, and an extremely popular innovation was Request Night. The programme for these shows was based on selections made by the patrons from the items included in the Epics' regular repertoire. An added attraction on these occasions was a lucky number draw. The programmes sold at the door were numbered, and a child was invited up from the audience to draw out the winning lucky numbers. The fortunate holders of the winning programmes were awarded Postal Orders. Doug Cranston was a naturally funny comedian and is reputed to have been capable of drawing a laugh from the most dour and puritanical minded members of his audience. Miss Delza also performed comic songs both solo and on occasion with Doug. Daisy Hellard, a soprano who was extremely popular with the Withernsea audiences, sang solos and also rendered duets with the company's tenor, Charles Charles.

Monty Burle was renowned for his act based on George Leybourne, the Lion Comique of the Music Halls. Leybourne was the swaggering, flamboyant man about town who immortalised the songs *Champagne Charlie* and *The Man on the Flying Trapeze*. Archie Barron provided able accompaniment on the piano for the troupe.

Grapho's Jovial Jollies of Saltburn fame were also frequent visitors to

*Bits o' Brightness, 1924, outside the Floral Hall Withernsea.*

**FLORAL HALL,**

Lessee : E. Grapho.    Manager : Sid Vance.

—

**BERT GRAPHO'S**

**" JOVIAL "**
**JOLLIES**

**"The Old Firm."**

—

**Thursday Night, September 5th,**

**BENEFIT**

TO

**LA TAGARTE**

AND

**TONY SPOORS.**

Book your seats at Nicholson's Music Shop.

*Playbill for 1929.*

*Bert Grapho's Jovial Jollies, 1929.*

Withernsea during this period. Originally the show was presented by Bert Grapho and after his death by his son Jack, ably assisted by Sid Vance who was Mrs Grapho's manager for the Withernsea season. Bert was in the process of finalising the arrangements for the 1929 shows when he died. Needless to say in the true tradition of entertainment the show did go on for the season. The people of Withernsea accorded a full measure of sympathy and respect to Mrs Grapho for her courageous gesture.

The Jovial Jollies performed on the beach daily on their alfresco near the end of Seaside Road. If wet they repaired to the Floral Hall, which was also the venue for evening shows on Thursdays and Saturdays and was always used for Benefit Nights. Over the years the company included such firm favourites as La Tagarte, Rita Moya, Beryl Fernandez, The Dubarry Sisters, Patsy and Ronnie, Arthur Carlton and Ernie Miller. The dancers included Jean Atkinson who was quite a favourite with the Saltburn audiences. Jessie Harrison who appeared in 1923 married a local man and made her home in Withernsea.

During the 1929 season, the 10th September was set aside for Ernie Miller's Benefit Night. Ernie, who was billed as a light comedian was celebrating his seventeenth consecutive season with the troupe. His wife, who was not a performer, sold tickets for the shows and guided people to their seats. There was an exceptionally large audience for the show (proof of Ernie's popularity) who were extremely generous with their gifts to mark the occasion. An additional attraction for the evening was the appearance of Mr. J.R. Stephenson of Hull who had a very fine bass voice and sang several songs. There was also a small band of juvenile dancers from Hull.

On September 23rd, almost at the end of the 1929 season, a Carnival Night concluding with a Snowball Fight was staged for Sid Vance's Benefit. Sid was very popular with the public. He had a reputation for unfailing courtesy and a genuine concern for the comfort of the patrons. He prided himself on presenting a good class of show, based on the precept of family entertainment, and was a real asset to Mrs Grapho after the death of Bert. He took part in the sketches and filled in with humorous cameos, in addition to carrying out his administrative duties. The season usually closed with a show entitled "Au Revoir Pierrot"; this as might be expected was a nostalgic performance which included popular items from the shows of the season.

Competitions were held for the children throughout the season, and were enthusiastically supported. One of our informants remembers the delight of gaining second prize in a competition for the longest hair. Tony Spoors was, of course, with the troupe on every occasion that they appeared in town. As previously mentioned he was with the company for many years, originally as pianist and later as musical director.

Jack Grapho was a favourite with the Withernsea audiences. The popular little comedian was referred to locally as "Our Jack". His Benefits were always packed to capacity, and the gifts were generous. The public loved his humorous songs and antics, and the applause was deafening, not only at the conclusion of his act but also for his appearance on stage. The show was basically a family concern, and as such knew how to appeal to families on the north east coast.

Mac's Supremes enjoyed a period of popularity and success in the town. The company was directed by Andrew McAllister (Mac), who began his career in entertainment, along with numerous other talented artistes, with Will Catlin at the turn of the century. Mac was a comedian, and his monologues, which were his speciality, were always enthusiastically received.

Ethel Ryder was the soprano and J. Clement Ellis the baritone, who in accepted manner performed solo items and duets. Elsie Sternake helped to provide the comedy along with Cyril Douglas who was also a pianist. Maude Selkirk was a soubrette and dancer and Terry Glynn a light comedian and dancer. This versatile pair also played saxophone, flute, piccolo and banjo. Obviously with so much talent available the programmes offered a variety of entertainment not often found in such a small group, and ensured immediate success.

The Lavender Club presented by Edgar Taylor returned time after time, by popular demand, to the town. Edgar was a light comedian and dancer, and Wynn Barton a comedienne. Daisy Hellard the soprano had already won the hearts of the residents during the time when she gave talented performances with Cranston's Epics in the town. Billy Roberts supplied the comedy, and there were two speciality artistes, dancer Joan Celia, and the other who was billed as "Scarperietta". All were ably accompanied on the piano by Dudley Downing.

The programme was designed to keep the audience involved throughout the show. It was a lively, swinging bill of non-stop entertainment, where singing, dancing, comedy and sketches were delivered with a high degree of professionalism. This was a novelty, obviously much appreciated by the patrons of the Floral Hall, who consistently filled the house for the company's shows.

Another group who were firm favourites in the twenties was Teddy Mann's Folly Folk. Over the years a number of artistes appeared with the company including such favourites as Ivy Le Claire soubrette and dancer, Alf Taylor, light comedian and dancer, Effie Patte, the Comedy Girl, Ethel Morton soprano, Henry Wilson baritone, Ray Rivers comedian, Vie Delmar soprano and Hilda Franks a violinist. Teddie himself was a pianist. During the 1929 season a Hull comedian Larry Teal appeared with the show, and proved very popular. Larry was at that time a much loved "Star" in the area.

The company usually consisted of seven artists. Ethel Morton and Henry Wilson performed solos and duets which were always received with enthusiasm. Ivy Le Clair and Alf Taylor danced duets which became a feature of the programme eagerly awaited by the audience. Effie Patte was famous for her child impressions and with Ray Rivers was responsible for the comedy side of the shows in which they appeared. Teddie Mann not only accompanied the shows on the piano and performed beautiful solos, but also wrote several of the numbers performed by the cast.

The Fun Employed appeared for a short season at the Floral Hall in 1929. There were alfresco matinees on the beach each day when fine. Mark Bennett and Kitt Walters were the directors of the show. Kitt, a female impersonator, delighted and amazed audiences with his remarkable singing and gorgeous gowns. Mark played the banjo and did character sketches, one of which called 'Grandfather's Dream' never failed to find popularity.

Ada Cadogan, a soprano, also sang duets with Kitt Walters. There was an extremely versatile male impersonator and comedienne Biddy Brewin; also Doris Dolores an accomplished dancer. They had an amazing musical team: Gladys Montague, a brilliant pianist and entertainer; Gordon Bennett, a violinist; and a Hawaiian Trio who played the Hawaiian guitar, banjos, lutes and violins. All this for the modest sum of 3d, 6d, and 1/- (children 1d) on the sands, or at the Floral Hall 3d, 6d, 1/-, 1/3 and 1/6 (children 3d, 6d and 9d). These prices are of course pre-decimal coinage.

No amount of entertainment in Withernsea would be complete without mention of a local dancer, Irene Lawson. As a teenager in 1933 Irene founded the Reldeen School of Dancing, and in the same year staged her first show at Unity Hall. She took the name of her venture from the firm for which she worked after leaving school, Needlers of Hull. Her first show was highly successful and every year since she has produced shows in the town, donating the proceeds to charity. She recently presented her 55th annual production.

During the early days, Irene regularly supplied dancers for the summer shows. A playbill for Ernie Payne's Footlight Revue at the Floral Hall lists Betty Fields (sister of the famous Gracie) and among others Irene Lawson's Twelve Dinky Dots. Other performers listed were the Two Taylors, Kitty and Billy a singing husband and wife duo, Lena Price, Mary Anderson, Doris Payne, Essie McLean, Kitty Rose, Sybil May, Billy Rose, Jack Buswell and lastly Ernie Payne, billed as "The Idol of Withernsea".

In 1932 Uncle Terry's Show Box, four men and five girls in traditional pierrot costume, gave an alfresco show accompanied by a pianist, and in 1936, Al Needham's Whirlwind Follies made an appearance in the town. The troupe consisted of six men and four girls with a combined, wide range of instrumental skills.

Charlie O'Neil who produced Pierrot Pie in 1938 was an experienced performer. He was associated with a number of shows between the wars, and was well known on the west coast, particulary at Morecambe and Grange-Over-Sands

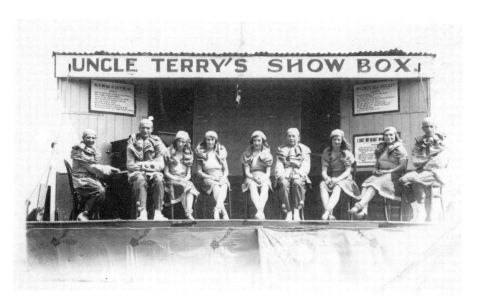

*Uncle Terry's Show Box, c.1932.*

*Al Needham's Whirlwind Follies. Needham is in suit and hat, centre.*

97

*Charlie O'Neill's Pierrot Pie, 1938 (Charlie in bowler hat).*

*The Hollym Follies.*

for his Wows Concert Party. The Withernsea company were eight in number, four men and four girls.

The Second World War virtually saw the end of the pierrots and seaside shows in Withernsea, as it did in other towns along the cost. Wartime restrictions put an end to seaside holidays as such for the duration; families were split up when the men joined the forces, some children were evacuated, and many women worked in various occupations where needed. The terrible Blitz on Hull shocked the whole of Holderness and the coastal area. In some of the towns there was an attempt at a Post-War revival (as related in previous chapters). The only troupe to approach the old-time pierrot shows in Withernsea were the Hollym Follies. They began in 1962 under the direction of Florence Coverdale who was President of the Hollym Branch of the Women's Institute and embarked upon what was to prove a long and successful career.

The original show was intended to provide entertainment for the annual Spurn Group Rally, and at this stage it is fair to say that none of the performers who admitted to being able to "dance a bit" or "sing a bit" envisaged a series of shows spanning almost twenty years.

There were seven dancers, Mary Talbot, Mary Carmichael, June Smith, Ena Stephenson, Clarice Briggs, Doreen Dennis and Doris Ledger. Doris was also responsible for the costumes. The vocalists were Gladys Stephenson and Johnnie Carmichael who achieved fame as a yodeller. Bill Ashwell and Phyllis Evans were the pianists and the company greatly valued the services of Lottie Tidswell, who was affectionately referred to as the "zipper upper".

The group enjoyed presenting their first show so much that they decided to continue and donate any proceeds to charity. A name now had to be found for the company. Flo's Follies was suggested, but the final choice came down in favour of The Hollym Follies, Hollym being a small village community about two miles south of Withernsea.

The troupe gave regular shows in Withernsea and the surrounding villages; their venues were many and varied from small village halls to the Grand Pavilion at Withernsea. They finally disbanded around the 1979-80 season, when sadly their numbers were depleted. The final blow came with the death of Bill Ashwell. During the years these dedicated performers, whose shows reached a very high standard, followed the pierrot tradition of bringing joy and happiness to many people in the area where they are still fondly remembered.

It would be fair to say that the "Beeching Axe" administered the "coup de grace" when the Hull to Withernsea line was closed. What had been for more than half a century a lively holiday town with an abundance of entertainment, was transformed into the friendly but quiet town we know today. The visitors are usually Sunday trippers from Hull, or visitors to the town's caravan sites during the summer season.

99

# ENVOI

## A TRADITION REVIVED

Even as we mourn the passing of the pierrots and concert parties along our Yorkshire coast, a new interest is being shown in the old style of entertainment. Groups of people are producing shows which though amateur in status are very professional in their presentation.

In most groups the old favourite songs are revived in preference to modern popular songs. Sketches and routines are again being presented in the manner of the pierrot tradition of yesteryear, and in one group at least the traditional pierrot costumes have been revived.

These groups are not producing one-off performances but are offering seasonal entertainment on the coast and like the pierrots are often willing to perform in the winter at other venues.

The organisers of these troupes, like the pierrot "Guvnors", work very hard, not only performing but also organising costumes, programmes and schedules.

In 1987, for the 150th Anniversary of Queen Victoria's accession to the throne, Saltburn held a Victorian celebration which included a Gala with street entertainment of the period and many other attractions. Veronica Twidle, herself an entertainer, who appeared with Dora Rayne's Follies at Aberystwyth in 1946/47 and also with other troupes during that period, presented "The End of the Pier Show". She wrote, produced and managed the show which was traditional in pierrot costume. This show proved so popular that Veronica is hoping to repeat the experiment during the summer of 1988.

The "ladies" of Bridlington began their enterprise a few years earlier. In December of 1982 Pauline Allman and Iris Christlow, two seaside landladies of Windsor Crescent decided they would like to put on a show for the holidaymakers in Bridlington.

They presented their idea to colleagues which culminated in a meeting of sixteen interested landladies at the Cock and Lion public house.

After the two originators elaborated on their proposal at length, a few others volunteered to help, and the manager of the pub, Jim Nixon, who had some previous experience in the entertainment field, promised to coach them. He choreographed the numbers, put them through strenuous routines and aimed for a high professional standard, which they ultimately achieved. He also organised singing lessons where required.

The object of the concert party was twofold. They wished to put Bridlington on the map, and any proceeds from the shows were to be donated to charity. The ladies have supported many worthy causes over the last few years. They called themselves the "Bridlington Bed and Breakfast Belles" and the original troupe included Pauline Allman and Iris Christlow, the two who conceived the idea, ably supported by Rosalind Johnson, Janice Cruddas, June Ellis, Pat Hyde and last, but by no means least, Joan Crowther. Joan is the comedienne of the troupe, and all are agreed the star of the show.

*The Bed & Breakfast Belles in the 1980's*

*The Jollybirds.*

101

The Belles now give a one hour show, which is in many ways similar to the original seaside entertainments. There is a great deal of enthusiasm and a lot of their material is spontaneous as they give of their best to entertain the public. They relate at length stories of primitive dressing rooms (or lack of) and there is an obvious cameraderie, which in itself ensures a good performance.

The Jollybirds began in 1973. They are Hull based but have performed on the coast at Hornsea and Withernsea. Originally they were a group of twelve ladies organised by Valerie Harrison, but have now been joined by the men. There are presently eight ladies and four men. The Jollybirds' production is in the style of the Old Time Music Hall. They are accompanied on the piano by Valerie who prefers this instrument to modern amplificiation, and there is a lot of audience participation in the chorus numbers. They have a wide repertoire which includes monologues, light classical duets, male and female comedy songs and an all male drag act, which they claim is "all good clean family entertainment".

The shows are extremely well dressed, each member taking a pride in their own and the collective appearance of the group. The men wear waistcoats and straw boaters, and on occasion, evening dress. The ladies are always appropriately dressed for the number being performed.

The present troupe are Valerie and Harold, Marion and George, May and Tom, Madge and Don, Maureen, Marion and Barbara, and their ages range from the 40's to 70's; one lady having reluctantly retired at the age of 80.

The main aim of the troupe is to bring pleasure to people, but any proceeds which result from their activities are donated to a worthy cause.

The Merrie Makers are based at Wakefield, and though not strictly a seaside show, we thought we must include them as their material and aims are very similar to the early pierrot seaside shows.

Specifically they work to bring pleasure to people with an emphasis on the elderly and sick, to whom they take their shows. No charge is made for their performances. The troupe was formed around 1979 and still has five of its original members. The present team consists of twelve, their ages ranging from twelve to sixty.

Nancy Goldthorpe, aided by Brenda Baker, produces the show. Again as in the early days of the concert party a piano is used as accompaniment. There is also Jean Owen a comedienne; May Whitaker does a mermaid routine and with Rosemary Ellis performs a duo act. They make all their own costumes and props and are agreed that their success is largely due to the fact that they are all good friends.

These are just a small sample of the groups who are preserving the old style of entertainment in Yorkshire. Judging from their popularity it is probably reasonable to hope for a revival of interest in the type of shows which gave much pleasure to our parents and grandparents.

*The Merrie Makers.*

# CATLIN MEN WHO APPEARED IN YORKSHIRE

Will Ambro (comedian)
Medley Barrett
Chas Beanland
Joe Beanland
Jackson Brown (singer)
Andie Caine (singer)
Tom Catlin (Braham Fox) (singer)
Will Catlin (Guvnor)
Clinton Carew
Reg Dayre (later Reg Howard) (comedian)
Arthur Ferris
Louis Finch (pianist)
F. Carlton Foster (singer)
Wilmot Fowler
Harold Franklin (female impersonator)
Willie Franklin (female impersonator)
Sid Frere (Director of Colwyn Bay) (tenor)
Golly Glynn (singer)
George Houghton (Director of Whitley Bay) (singer, comedian)
Tom Lewis
Albert Lyon (singer)
Bert Lytton (singer)
Billie Manders (female impersonator)
Andrew McAllister
Will B. Merry
Charles Milner (Director Withernsea)
Harry Mitchell-Craig (Director of Llandudno) (singer)
Ernie Preston
Kemsley Scott-Barrie (comedian, female impersonator)
Frank A. Terry (baritone, dancer)
Ernest Tilbury
Harry Vernon
Teddy Weeton

# GLOSSARY OF TERMS

| | |
|---|---|
| *Alfresco* | Meaning literally "in the open air". Used in reference to the stage set up on the beach by the pierrots. |
| *Arcadia* | Literally "an ideal place". Used to describe the small wooden theatre-like structures built by some more prosperous pierrot troupes. |
| *Barrer Man* | The man who pushed the piano or strill to the beach on a handcart or "barrer" for the pierrots. |
| *Benefit Night* | A night on which the proceeds were given to a named member of the troupe, each member taking a turn in rotation. Gifts were often presented by members of the public to their favourite performers. |
| *Black Face* | or Blacking Up. Crude make-up used by minstrels for effect. It was made from burnt cork soaked in water and applied to the skin. |
| *Bones* | "Mr Bones" or sometimes "Uncle Bones". A main member of a minstrel troupe, usually a comedian. |
| *Bottling* | Method of collecting money from the non-paying spectators watching the performance. Fully described in the introduction. |
| *Character Man* | Usually a comedian who did a speciality act or sketch based on a character, such as a Chelsea Pensioner or other distinctive person. |
| *Feed* | The person who supplies the principal comedian with cues. |
| *Guv'nor* | Affectionate term applied to the man in charge of the show. |
| *Mr. Interlocutor* | Compere of a minstrel show. Literally one who takes part in a dialogue or conversation, famous for "I say, I say" jokes. |
| *Pitch* | The place where a performer or entertainer actually does his act. Usually used consistently by minstrels and pierrots. |
| *Sketch* | A small situation comedy with an interchange of jokes and dialogue between members of the troupe. |
| *Skull Cap* | A black silk square or handkerchief tied around the head by pierrots, usually surmounted by a conical hat. |
| *Soubrette* | Light comedienne, who usually put over her act in a pert or cheeky manner. |

106

| | |
|---|---|
| *Strill* | A portable harmonium popular with some of the early pierrot troupes. |
| *Taking the Curtain* | Appearing on stage for the last curtain of the show. |
| *Tambo Man* | The man who shakes the tambourine in the minstrel show to punctuate the remarks of Mr. Interlocutor. |
| *White Face* | The type of make-up used by the early pierrots to complete the black and white illusion. This was a particularly obnoxious concoction made from zinc and lard. Some pierrots also favoured patches and enhanced the look by applying them to their cheekbones and chin. |

# BIBLIOGRAPHY

## BOOKS

Adamson, Simon. *Seaside Piers,* Batsford, 1977.
Mee, Arthur. *Yorkshire, North Riding,* Hodder & Stoughton, 1941.
Mee, Arthur. *Yorkshire, East Riding,* Hodder & Stoughton, 1941.
Mellor, Geoff. *Pom Poms and Ruffles,* Dalesman, 1966.
Mellor, Geoff. *Northern Music Halls,* Howe Bros, Gateshead, 1970.
Pitman. *Who's Who in the Theatre* (Various years).
Pulling, Christopher. *They Were Singing,* Harrap, London 1952.
Rose, Clarkson. *Beside the Seaside,* Museum Press, 1960.
Short, E with Compton Rickett, A. *Ring up the Curtain,* Herbert Jenkins, 1938.
Short, Ernest. *Fifty Years of Vaudeville,* Eyre & Spottiswoode, 1946.
Short, Ernest. *Sixty Years of Theatre,* Eyre & Spottiswoode, 1951.

## NEWSPAPERS (Early editions researched)

Bridlington Free Press
Hull Times
Redcar and Saltburn News
Scarborough Mercury
Whitby Gazette
Withernsea Gazette

## SOUVENIR BOOKLET

Memorial of German East Coast Raids and Bombardment, 1915.